BECOMING BETTER GROWNUPS

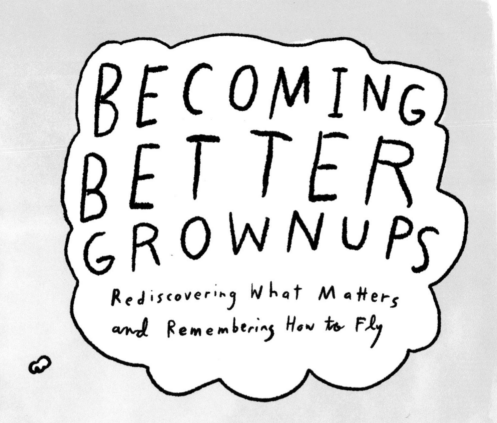

BECOMING BETTER GROWNUPS

Rediscovering What Matters and Remembering How to Fly

WRITTEN AND ILLUSTRATED BY

Brad Montague

AVERY
an imprint of Penguin Random House
New York

A
AVERY

An imprint of Penguin Random House LLC
penguinrandomhouse.com

Most Avery books are available at special quantity discounts for bulk
purchase for sales promotions, premiums, fund-raising, and educational
needs. Special books or book excerpts also can be created to fit specific
needs. For details, write SpecialMarkets@penguinrandomhouse.com.

Library of Congress Cataloging-in-Publication Data
Names: Montague, Brad, author.
Title: Becoming better grownups : rediscovering what matters and
remembering how to fly / written and illustrated by Brad Montague.
Description: New York : Avery, 2020.
Identifiers: LCCN 2019039064 (print) | LCCN 2019039065 (ebook) |
ISBN 9780525537847 (hardcover) | ISBN 9780525537854 (epub)
Subjects: LCSH: Adulthood. | Conduct of life.
Classification: LCC HQ799.95 .M66 2020 (print) |
LCC HQ799.95 (ebook) | DDC 305.24—dc23
LC record available at https://lccn.loc.gov/2019039064
LC ebook record available at https://lccn.loc.gov/2019039065
p.   cm.

Printed in China
1   3   5   7   9   10   8   6   4   2

Book design by Ashley Tucker

For my family

"I'M NOT GETTING OLDER,
I'M GETTING BETTER."

—Dorothy,
a woman I met who'd just turned 88

AUTHOR'S NOTE

This book is a work of love, which
was written just for you.
And I am happy to report
the stories found within are true.
However, in some cases—
parents, children, and schools, you see—
the names have been changed
to protect all privacy.

TABLE of CONTENTS

I don't know the exact moment they allowed me to begin sitting at the grownups' table. I do know I have yet to feel comfortable at it.

Growing up! It seemed like a good idea. Actually, it seemed like a great idea. Grownups have keys to cars, they can eat ice cream anytime they want, and they have all the answers. All of them.

Answers were something I wanted, and something I'm still wanting.

It all seemed so simple. Growing up would just happen to me. I had it all figured out: One day I would wake up and enter the kingdom of adulthood. Magically, this transition would be accompanied with facial hair, knowledge of tax laws, and a keen ability to find great deals, parking spaces, and difficult answers to crossword puzzles. Basically, I would know everything. Absolutely everything.

Cue high school graduation. Nothing. I walk the stage a bit wiser, I think. I touch my face—only minimal beard growth. Definitely no knowledge of tax laws. I come to the conclusion that my adulthood superpowers just haven't quite kicked in yet. Cue

college graduation: same. Marriage? Lovely, but now there are two of us who don't have it all figured out. Cue children—and this is when, for me, panic really begins to set in. Now there are other little humans being brought into this mess and no answers. None.

I need those magic grownup powers. Maybe you do, too?

Before we go any further, it's only proper that I let you know something: I am no expert. There, I said it. In fact, when it comes to most things, I'm what some might call gloriously inept. To ease my conscience I've pulled together a short, and by no means comprehensive, list of things I'm not great at (see facing page).

Now that that's out of the way, I can let you know that I'm at least trying to be great at one thing: being a grownup. Despite my best efforts, I am what some would refer to as a "grownup."* I still

---

*In this book I'll be referring to all adults, former kids, and chronologically older humans as *grownups*. I'll be using the unhyphenated version of the word because, upon investigating, I discovered that you spell this as either *grown-up* or *grownup*. I decided to follow the lead of authors Stan and Jan Berenstain, since they used the unhyphenated version in their 1992 *The Berenstain Bears and the Trouble with Grownups*.

A FEW THINGS BRAD CAN'T DO
(PARTIAL LIST ONLY)

MATH

EAT WITH A FORK

ATHLETICS

FIND CAR KEYS

SIT IN CHAIR

ORGANIZE CLOSETS

PRONOUNCE "GIF" CORRECTLY

FIND CAR KEYS
(seriously. If you see them let me know.)

BUTTON SHIRTS PROPERLY

OPEN BOXES

ROLL TONGUE

WORK HEAVY MACHINERY

SPREADSHEETS

FITTED SHEETS

REMEMBER PASSWORDS

FIND CAR
(HEY, I found my keys. Not sure where I parked.)

YOGA WITHOUT LAUGHING

DIRECTIONS

EVEN (as in "CAN'T EVEN")

and the newly discovered:
BEGIN A BOOK WITHOUT
WRITING SOMETHING EMBARRASSING

can't help strongly relating to Antoine de Saint-Exupéry's words in *The Little Prince*, though. He says, "I have lived a great deal among grown-ups. I have seen them intimately, close at hand. And that hasn't much improved my opinion of them." True words, right? There are many who give being a grownup a really bad look. You're already thinking of names. Be nice.

ANTOINE de SAINT-EXUPÉRY
(author, pilot, good grownup)

For me, it was shortly after discovering I would be a father that I dubbed my life Operation Be a Better Grownup. It was a wake-up call. This meant stepping up and becoming the dad I'd always promised myself I'd be. This meant becoming fully alive so that I could truly make this tiny new life proud. This meant coming to terms with the fact that I had no idea what to do next.

I feverishly set out to learn from anyone and everyone what it might mean to be a better adult human person. I began listening more, something I wasn't necessarily great at. I spent time with young people and old people. I confronted what it might mean to be a bad grownup. I questioned the virtues of maybe being just a boring grownup. Best of all, though, I began to dream about what it might look like to be a great grownup. The kind of grownup I'd always wanted to become. The kind of grownup I'd forgotten I could be. The kind of grownup that the kids of the world need us to be.

It's been both refreshing and frightening to discover that most of the adults I once looked to for guidance felt as clueless as I currently do. I spent years leaning on them for advice on how to do this life thing, and the whole time they also had no clue where to put their salad fork, either. That fourth-grade teacher who trans-

formed the way I see the world and myself in it? She was a scared, new teacher just trying to figure it all out. That mentor I go to so often for advice on how to be fulfilled in my family and career? He's trying to make sense of his place on this planet, too. My mother, who nurtured me, inspired me, and loved me into being? She was an overjoyed and terrified young woman, and I was her first child.

Growing up, just like breaking up, can be very hard to do.

This book is the result of hundreds of conversations with thousands of people, young and old, about becoming a better grownup. It began as a project focusing only on children's ideas about growing up, but evolved to include my discussions on adulthood with actual grownups. Those in both the morning and the twilight of their lives have a lot to teach us about what it means to grow and mature. These people don't always get the microphone, but this journey taught me just how much that needs to change. Each chapter focuses on key insights I've learned from listening to kids and

former kids. I am indebted to the many educators in classrooms, assisted-living centers, and hospitals who opened up time in their already crowded schedules. These wise souls helped shape this book and, with no exaggeration, my life.

One thing great grownups do is tell bedtime stories. This book, however, is not a bedtime story. Bedtime stories are told out of a desire to lull a little one to sleep. Within bedtime stories we hide little pieces of goodness to help children in their waking hours. We tuck important lessons into these stories about sharing, telling the truth, and overcoming fear. But at the end of the day—and that's when these are told—bedtime stories are really meant to reassure, calm, and get the young listeners to just go to sleep already.

I share this story, and this book, because it is a wake-up story. It is about my attempt to become a real-life, wide-awake grownup person. It is about how listening for wisdom woke me up. I asked questions and then did this thing that was fairly new to me, in which I actually listened to the responses. What I heard made me completely reimagine my adult life.

In spite of my uneasiness at being a grownup, I keep showing up. On the day my daughter was born, I held her. I'm told that each day, across the world, nearly 350,000 babies are born. That day, one of 350,000 new bundles of light in the world was handed to me. *Me*. There I stood, feeling a feeling that I've come to associate with being an adult: the feeling of being both gigantic and oh so very small. This new little baby girl looked up at me.

What did she do?

She laughed.

I melted.

I recalled this moment to friends and loved ones later and they all unanimously agreed—it was gas. But I knew better. That little laugh was packed with hope and possibility. In spite of all my inadequacies and all my feelings of unworthiness, she laughed. This little girl entered the world and then my arms and then she immediately laughed. Having just accomplished one of the most remarkable feats any living thing can do—*entering the world*—she laughed. In the face of grand beauty and mystery, she laughed. Maybe we could all do the same.

In moments big and small, she has continued to laugh, affirming my suspicions that it really was more than just gas. There's such a joyful lightness to her that, at times, I remain fearful she'll simply float away. This led to the inspiration for a story included throughout this book, "The Incredible Floating Girl." It's a simple tale told in three parts, and it frames the book's beginning, middle, and end. It's not a bedtime story. It's a wake-up story.

At this moment, we're the grownups in the room. For just a few short heartbeats, blinks, and breaths, we get to be here. My hope is that this book inspires more moments of childlike joy for you. Holding my daughter that first day and hearing her laugh, I was overwhelmed by the exuberance. In that moment, my heart and mind were not occupied with the burden of adulthood. I was simply focused on the thrill and beauty of becoming a better grownup. Whatever your role or wherever you may find yourself, I hope this book inspires you to do the same. Secretly, also, my hope is that one day in the far-off future, should my children find themselves also scratching their heads about growing up, they'll find this book right when they need it, read these stories, and remember.

While there is much I don't know, one thing has become increasingly certain for me: Being a better grownup has a whole lot to do with being more like a child. We become fully alive when we listen to the child within us and the children around us. Our work, our ideas, our to-do lists, everything in our wake—it all changes when we view it as a child does. We become softer, kinder, and, yes, sillier. I'm convinced a life lived like this can create a more helpful and hopeful world for kids and former kids everywhere.

Here's to better grownups. May we be them. May we raise them.

To the possibilities,

BRAD

the incredible floating girl
(A STORY IN THREE PARTS)

part one

FIRST FLIGHT

May I share with you a story?
It is wild and it is true.
Believe me when I say this:
there was once a girl who flew.

It didn't make the papers.
In fact, afraid some might
call them fakers,
they tried to keep it
from their neighbors.
So nobody around them had a clue.

She was just a few months old
when her dad put her to bed.

And—laughing—up she went
and on the ceiling hit her head.

He caught her safely
but was still in disbelief.
He tried to tell his wife, but she said,
"Dear, you need more sleep."

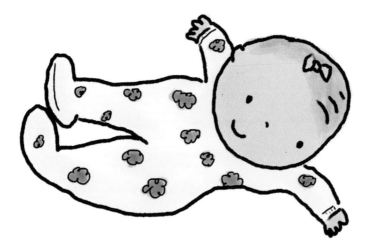

Sure enough, it happened again.
And her dad said, "See!
Every time I come near this girl,
she loses her gravity!"

Smiling wide and laughing loud,
up, up, up, she'd go.
And there he would stand terrified
and shaking down below.

"I will catch you! I will catch you!
Please get down here!" he'd cry.
But she only floated higher
when her father was nearby.

Floating runs in all families.
How it works, we do not know.
And I'm sorry here to add that
you forget how as you grow.

C H A P T E R
O N E

R A I S E Y O U R H A N D
I F Y O U
A R E H E R E

"Y'all need to wake up."

These were the words of a young girl named Marissa. She and her fourth-grade class were sharing with me a list of things they wanted grownups to know. I'd asked these students to be honest with their feedback, and they did not pull any punches. My promise to Marissa's class was the same promise I'd go on to give to every classroom I'd visit along the way: that these suggestions would be passed along by me to the grownup world. For Marissa, as for many of the students I spent time with, knowing that her words might be presented to the older humans of the planet brought out a deep sense of urgency. When she spoke up, she did so with great conviction. The sly smile on her face seemed to suggest she strongly believed that her words might rattle the status quo. With all the sass this young girl could muster, she looked at me and said, "Y'all need to wake up."

So, grownups: Y'all need to wake up. Marissa said so. Just passing this along.

I set a goal of listening to at least one elementary school classroom in each of the fifty states. I even gave this a name: the Listening Tour. The response from schools was so positive that there was no shortage of people willing to join me in this odd little project. Then, to complicate things further, I discovered how much I loved doing it. It quickly went from fifty classrooms to more than one hundred.

The Listening Tour wasn't about me visiting schools with something to share. Normally when people go on tour, they have something to perform or present. With this project, I was essentially touring as a one-man audience member. My job was to listen, while also occasionally throwing out some questions. With every question, I discovered just how much children had to share. Questions focused on what they thought of grownups, what kind of grownup they wanted to become, and, of course, how grownups could be better. The answers were as diverse as the students and the learning environments from which they came. Sometimes they were vague: "Grownups should be cool." When I asked exactly how to do that, one girl replied, "You know, *cool.*" I wish I did, but sadly, I do not know cool.

Sometimes the responses were much longer. One student named Hayden was inspired to write "The Declaration of Kidependence":

I declare the freedom of kids, because adults mistreat us because of our age. We the kids should be treated with respect as adults have for each other. We the kids should have fun, because all work (school) and no play is no way to live. We the kids, 0–18 years old, should be loved and be treated nicely, for we have only a limited amount of time before adulthood. We the kids want rights! We want freedom!

His mom told me that Hayden had hung it on his bedroom door at home, like a modern-day Martin Luther nailing his Ninety-Five Theses on the church door. Doesn't that belong in a film? Can't you just hear the music swelling? It's a pretty audacious and stylish way to deliver your message. The first time I saw this, I laughed. But the more I thought about it, the more I envied this kid's passion and daring. I want to live with that same sort of spirit. There was a time when I did express myself and my emotions in such big ways, but adulthood muted that. This book, I guess you could say, is my note on the bedroom door. I'm just trying to be like Hayden.

In the end I listened to more than one hundred conversations in classrooms across the United States. They revealed so much about a wide array of topics, but overwhelmingly, a few common themes emerged. And there was one giant theme that refused to go away. From classroom to classroom, visit to visit, interview to interview, time and again it

> The Declaration of Kidependence
>   I declare the freedom of kids, because adults mistreat us because of our age. We the kids should be treated with respect as adults have for each other. We the kids should have fun, because work (school) and no play is no way to live. We the kids, 0–18 years old, should be loved and be treated nicely, for we have only a limited amount of time before adulthood. We the kids want rights! We want freedom!
>   Hayden

became abundantly clear: Kids want grownups to be present. This wish echoed in the words of Marissa, as she asked that we "wake up," and in the requests of nearly every single child I spent time with. It was a request from children spoken sometimes between the lines, sometimes subtly, sometimes loudly, and sometimes even with these exact two little words: *Show up.*

So, what does it mean to show up? To really show up in the world?

There is a great ritual that takes place every day in schools all over. It might be referred to by lots of different names in other places, but when I was in elementary school, it was known as roll call. The teachers would take attendance by going down the list of students' names alphabetically. Each student would then have to raise their hand when their name was called and say, "Present."

Though some days I didn't want to be there, I did not want to be counted absent. I had, after all, gone to the trouble of getting out of bed, braving the hallway, and making it to that desk. I was going to make my presence known. Put a check mark by my name, teacher. I am present.

There isn't really any sort of attendance-accountability equivalent in the adult world. People do tend to take notice when you skip work or miss a meeting. Some workplaces have time clocks where you punch in on arrival. However, in very few instances do grownups have to raise their hands and their voices and announce to everyone, "I am present."

So, can we do a roll call? Where are the grownups? Are you here?

Show up. This was my first big lesson on the Listening Tour. In fact, it's sort of how the Listening Tour got started—except it was more like someone else decided I was going to show up. I'd just become a new parent. I'd spent a long stretch of time working non-stop. I was tired. More specifically, I was burned out. Well, not just burned out. Things had gotten so bad that some days I would show up to my office and just lie down on the floor. For the first time in my life I'd started seeing a counselor and for the first time heard words like "anxiety" and "depression" used in sentences that were about me. My plans for new projects were not working out. I had no clue what to do next. I felt like I was at the bottom of a well and couldn't get out. Then a teacher emailed me.

The request was from Mrs. B and her third-grade class. She and her students had been working on group projects, and as part of their grade, they needed to present their idea to an adult. Mrs. B

chose me because these projects had been done in response to something I'd posted online. In a video, I'd asked people to finish this sentence: *The world would be more awesome if* _____. Her third graders had formed into groups and dreamed up ways to fill in that blank. All I'd have to do was connect with them from my laptop at home, listen, and provide a bit of positive feedback.

While I certainly felt honored—and also very curious as to what their ideas for making the world more awesome might be— I had serious reservations about saying yes. First, these young, hope-filled hearts didn't need a tired, burned-out old guy. I mean, I'm not old per se. However, to most third graders, anyone over ten is ancient. Second, I had another pretty good excuse. It was an old one that I'd brought out time and time again: *There are plenty of better grownups for this task.*

Maybe you've done this before, too? I often convince myself that I'm not a real grownup and that other people are. These other real people have it all figured out. I, on the other hand, am a fraud. I am a giant child who, because he's had the right number of birthdays, has suddenly been given ridiculous amounts of responsibility. When I'm tapped on the shoulder to do something, like chat with a group of elementary school students, my first thought is, *They're making a mistake.*

There's something I've been learning, though. Better grownups do not believe that they should just wait around for other better grownups to show up. There might be people around who are more skilled at budgeting than you are. There might be people around who are more experienced at building than you are. There might be people around who are more trained to do any number of things better than you can. Please know this: No one is better suited to be you than you. You are perfectly cast in your role, and we need you. Children need you. The world needs you.

Even though they might feel inadequate, great grownups show up. So, show up. Show up. Show up.

In true tenacious-teacher fashion, Mrs. B stuck with me. When I didn't respond to her first email, she reached out again. When I responded to her second email with a "maybe," she responded with a "here's what time it's happening" email. Well, okay then.

The time came to connect with Mrs. B's classroom, and I was uneasy. Looking back, it's so ridiculous. This required very little on my part. I didn't have to prepare anything. I didn't even have to leave my house. The stakes could not have been lower. My only job was to listen to kids and be supportive. How I'd allowed myself to get to a point where that seemed stressful, I'll never fully understand. Sometimes insecurities can scream so loudly that you become unable to hear all the great possibilities whispering underneath them. I really believed that a better grownup should be doing this instead of me. This classroom visit, and the more than one hundred that would follow, showed me otherwise.

When my laptop screen first lit up with the students' faces, there was giddy laughter. After some excessive waving and a brief introduction, Mrs. B gave the go-ahead to one of the groups. Little bundles of students would rise up and unveil their dreams for a better world. "The world would be better if there were no bullying," they said. Then they'd proceed to show how they could address that issue in their school. One group talked about creating recycling stations. Another shared their plans for getting canned foods donated to people in their community. This was real-deal stuff they were doing. I was blown away.

Before I knew it, our time was up. Schedules are tight in the world of classrooms, and they had to move along. The call concluded just as it had begun, with a few dozen third graders all smiling and waving. I waved back, thanked them, and tried not to let them see me get emotional. I hadn't realized how much I'd needed to hear their hopefulness. My screen went dark, and I sat in silence, stunned.

From that moment, I was hooked. I began trying to figure out how I could keep learning from students. I wanted to hear more of their hopes and dreams. I wanted the grownup world to hear them, too. I thought maybe their zest for life and doing good could rub off on everyone. It was all too contagious in the best sort of way. Though so much else in my life at that time seemed uncertain, I suddenly had one thing I knew for sure: Everyone needed to hear from kids.

Once I'd decided to embark on this quest, I emailed a link for people to apply to be part of the Listening Tour. I sent it to a small group of teachers, but educators can be a generous bunch. They passed the information about this project all over the world. This led to more than 3,000 classrooms applying, about 2,950 more than I had anticipated. Again, proof that if you want something to happen, just enlist a team of caring teachers.

The response from kids was an enthusiastic one, too. They were excited to be given the microphone, but even more than that, they were thrilled to know that their ideas and thoughts would be shared. Whether by video call or in person, every classroom greeted me warmly and then immediately launched into expressing their challenging, hilarious, and often profound insights on what it means to be a person in the world. I quickly discovered how people come alive when you listen to them. This is true of kids *and* grownups. We all long to be seen and heard. From the very first classroom visit and onward, I was given a lesson in how listening can change everything.

When I asked children, "What does a good grownup look like?" they told me things like this:

"A good grownup is always there for you, even when you mess up." —Sydney

"They support you. They come to stuff like plays and games." —Logan

"I think a good grownup is someone you can always count on." —Brendan

"They show up to stuff." —Courtney

"A good grownup does things with you that are fun and also helps you when you have to do things that aren't fun." —Mischa

"Somebody who is there all the time." —Nicholas

When I reframed the question as "What do you want from the grownups in your life?" they gave similar answers:

"I want them to stop worrying about things and smile and let's all just be happy together." —Gabrielle

"It'd be cool if we went on lots of adventures. Like maybe we could go somewhere together?" —Jacob

"I just think they could be nicer and funner. I want them to play around and talk with me. Maybe play games. I don't know." —Lydia

"They need to get off their phones." —Theo

"I want all my grownups to do things with me and have fun." —Natalie

Dr. Junlei Li is a senior lecturer in early childhood education at the Harvard Graduate School of Education. I often look to him for guidance not only because he is incredibly intelligent but also because he cares deeply about children. He pointed out to me that the students were all reflecting something research has been getting wise to. Kids really do want and need grownups who can be present; the National Scientific Council on the Developing Child in 2004 described relationships as the "active ingredients"* in

---

* National Scientific Council on the Developing Child, *Young Children Develop in an Environment of Relationships: Working Paper No. 1* (2004). Retrieved from www.developingchild.harvard.edu.

healthy development. In 2015, Harvard University's Center on the Developing Child released a paper on the resilience of children that stated, "The single most common finding is that children who end up doing well have had at least one stable and committed relationship with a supportive parent, caregiver, or other adult."* Reminders that relationships are where the real treasure lies. Present, engaged, loving grownups are vital to helping kids learn and grow.

Years ago I put this in a video. I had my young brother-in-law, Robby, play the part of a kid who thought he was in charge of the world. I called it *Kid President*. Nine years old and wearing a suit, he stood and spoke directly to the camera: "It's science: You're here. You take up space. You matter." It was a silly joke, and I wrote it to be an encouraging, self-esteem-boosting vote of confidence for whoever might be watching. I always assumed it'd be mostly young people watching. It's a message I wanted every young person to know, so I made it central to nearly every video.

---

*Center on the Developing Child at Harvard University, *Supportive Relationships and Active Skill-Building Strengthen the Foundations of Resilience: Working Paper No. 13* (2015). Retrieved from www.developingchild.harvard.edu.

You matter. I'd said it to so many other people and forgotten to say it to myself. I'm growing to understand that there's so much more to the way we matter to one another than I'd ever known. We need each other. Somehow, your presence and my presence forever impact the world around us.

Each time students gave me actual names of good grownups in their lives, they would smile giant smiles. They spoke of teachers. They spoke of family members. They mentioned neighbors and family friends. They told stories of small moments, like "We go to the park every Saturday together" or "We eat dinner at my grandma's every Sunday," which were all very big deals to them. Dr. Anne K. Fishel, an associate clinical professor of psychology at Harvard Medical School, has been gathering research over the past few years that actually shows the massive impact sharing a meal can have. She started the Family Dinner Project as a way to help spread that message. One study from Columbia University found that eating dinner with their family five days a week can drastically change the life of children. Everything from lower levels of substance abuse to higher grade-point averages and stronger self-esteem were correlated with kids' spending small amounts of quality time with caring grownups in their lives.[*] When grownups are fully present, children feel heard, seen, and valued. When children feel heard, seen, and valued, anything is possible. Beautiful things happen.

It was obvious to me when I was speaking to a child who felt heard, seen, and valued. There was a confidence and a brightness. They spoke freely of the people who were in their midst who believed in them. It was also obvious when the child was hungry for a caring presence in their lives.

---

[*] CASAColumbia, *The Importance of Family Dinners VI* (2010). Retrieved from https://www.centeronaddiction.org/addiction-research/reports/importance-of -family-dinners-2010.

I know my caring presence can be important. Yet so often I've felt like I was not the right grownup for the job. With my own children, I've felt inadequate. I've wished I were a more confident dad, the kind of parent they deserve. As I found myself in classrooms, I quietly agonized over my deficiencies as a grownup. I wished I were the kind of grownup I thought they needed.

Once I visited with a group of third graders on the West Coast. As the students gathered on a rug in the center of their classroom to sit crisscross applesauce, I sat in a chair. I'm sure regular stretching and a better diet might make it possible for me to sit crisscross applesauce, but it seems like a lot of effort to put in just for the ability to sit on the floor. Chairs exist for a reason, and I am a fan of chairs.

Seated beside me were a few fellow grownups. (They were also in chairs.)

We'd all been gathered to talk with these third graders about what we do. To alleviate any stress about what to expect during our classroom visit, the teacher wrote in an email to each of us, "Just be yourself." While I appreciated the spirit of her thought, at that moment, seated in that chair, I would've preferred to be anyone else.

POLICE OFFICER   VETERINARIAN   ELECTED OFFICIAL   ME

The other adults assembled were a police officer, a veterinarian, and an elected official of some sort. Her title was repeated several times but, with apologies to this elected official, I could never quite figure out exactly what she did. Though it was clear to me that she was super-important. In addition to the long title, she was nicely dressed, causing me to look down uncomfortably at my jeans and untucked shirt. Yet another reason to feel completely out of my element.

The teacher started by introducing the police officer, saying a few words about who she was and what she did. She explained that the students might want to be a police officer one day. Then she did the same for the veterinarian. And then for the elected official.

As she introduced the others, I thought, *Oh no. Please don't tell these students that. They do not want to be like me. I can barely eat with a fork, and my car smells like cat pee.*

Every part of me cringed as I awaited my introduction. I began to daydream about other career options. I wished I could be the police officer. Serving. Protecting. Wearing a cool uniform. I envied the veterinarian. The kids in the room were going to love him. I'd love to work with animals, but by "work with" I mean pet them when I want to and let someone else feed and clean them. My inner critic interrupted. These were not real grownup thoughts.

I wanted to be able to appear proudly before these children and be anyone other than who I really was. Even now I wish I could write to all of you reading this book that I'm an astronaut or a deep-sea diver. I wish I could tell you that I'm some exotic sailor or a regular sailor or even a human with a boat. I am none of those things. I'm a writer and a doodler. I create short videos for web and television. Basically, I make things people pass around on the internet. I did not belong in that seat. Yet I was introduced to these children as a possible version of their future.

Remarkably, I was able to refrain from doing anything too embarrassing as the teacher turned her attention to me. I told them more about what I did. I didn't wet my pants. I considered this a win.

I was relieved when, just as I'd expected, most of the kids had questions for the veterinarian. All the kids wanted to know about animals. Even I asked him some questions. Anything to keep the focus away from my little work in the world.

Then a small hand in the back rose up and a quiet voice spoke.

"What were you like as a kid?"

The boy asking the question nodded his head toward me as he said it. My eyes opened wide, and I pointed to myself.

"Me?" I asked.

"Yes," he said in a timid voice.

Before I could respond, the teacher excitedly interrupted. "This is Marcus. He's the artist in our classroom." She pointed to some of his work on the wall, and he blushed.

With that bit of information, it became clear why Marcus had asked me that question. Being the quiet, art-minded kid in the back of the class at one time myself, I could feel all his many reasons for gathering the courage to speak. He didn't really want to know about me and my childhood. He wanted to know if it was okay for

him to be the artist in the class. He wanted to know if it was okay to be the kid he is now and the kind of grownup he's headed toward becoming. He wanted some sort of reassurance that he didn't have to stop being who he was. He wanted to know that he was okay.

Feeling that, knowing that, I began to tell him what I was like as a kid. Then I proceeded to do everything I could to let him know he was more than okay. The compliments came easily. I did not have to pretend. The raw talent of this young boy was obvious, and so was his artistic desire. Yet I could sense all that might be ahead for him—the doubting, the struggles. Maybe one day he'd even find himself, as I was, seated alongside fellow grownups, each with different talents. Maybe he'd find himself feeling out of place. I wanted him to feel anything but that. So I let him know that his voice and gifts were desperately needed in this world, just as all voices and gifts are.

"Stay you, Marcus," I said. "Stay you."

It was a lesson I also needed to tell myself.

Afterward, the teacher sent me a drawing Marcus had done. He'd put two birds in the sky and written the words "Thank you." Along with it was a note from the teacher about how much that day had meant to him. Neither she nor Marcus truly had any clue just how much that day had meant to me, too. That interaction played over and over in my head the entire trip home and continued to stick with me.

Sitting in that classroom, I'd been wishing I were someone else, but, as it turned out, I was exactly who I needed to be.

You'd think a magical moment like that with Marcus would've ingrained this lesson in my head and heart. If only. By the time other teachers reached out with requests for me to visit their classrooms, I'd long forgotten. One thing that really does come along with getting older is a sort of forgetfulness that is far worse than misplacing your car keys or misremembering your email passwords. We seem to develop an addiction to distraction that can make us forget who we really are. And when you don't know who you are, you can't be where you are. Showing up can become an impossible task.

Before classroom visits, I found myself writing, "BE PRESENT. BE PRESENT. BE PRESENT . . ." Back when I was in school, as punishment, teachers would sometimes require you to write something over and over, until either you learned your lesson or your hand fell off. Now as I was writing "BE PRESENT" for the thousandth time, I was my own authority figure attempting to instill this newly learned lesson that I did not want to forget. I would be present and accounted for. This would spill over from how I operated in classrooms visits to how I lived my life.

One of the superpowers children have is the ability to exist fully in the moment. What is a toddler if not a human swept away and overcome by everything life has to offer? From colors and sounds to textures and tastes, small children are wide awake to the world around them.

Mix this with newly discovered abilities like walking and talking and getting reactions from bigger humans, and it's a recipe for a person fully present.

Maybe this is why time seems to move at a snail's pace when we're children. Birthdays and Christmases seem as if they're ages away and will never arrive. Each moment is loaded with so much to experience and to process. Children are so deeply rooted in the magic of the everyday that time is both abundant and completely stalled. There's a full magic show going on all the time, but we grow up and get too busy to pay attention to it.

During classroom visits, kids would lean forward in their chairs. Their eyes were wide and their hands were open. They were quick to chime in with their thoughts, but just as quick to hear what classmates had to share. It was an active listening, a way of conversing that I tried to copy. Though our visits would often be short, I was always amazed at how much could be packed into such a brief time. Their full immersion in the moment left no space wasted. They were present and, by being so, taught me how to be present, too.

The more I listened to children, the more I learned about time. The more I learned about time, the more I wanted to change how I engaged with it. I let the tick of the clock slip away and just fully engaged with students. I noticed more. My worries about whatever else was on my schedule for the day would fade, allowing my brain to focus on the faces in front of me. The noisy insecurities so often barking in my ear began to quiet down. I stopped being worried about what to say next. Instead, I became concerned with fully being there, just the way a child is.

Kids want and need grownups who will be present. Better grownups don't wait around for a better grownup. They just show up.

CHILD BRAIN:

GROWNUP BRAIN:

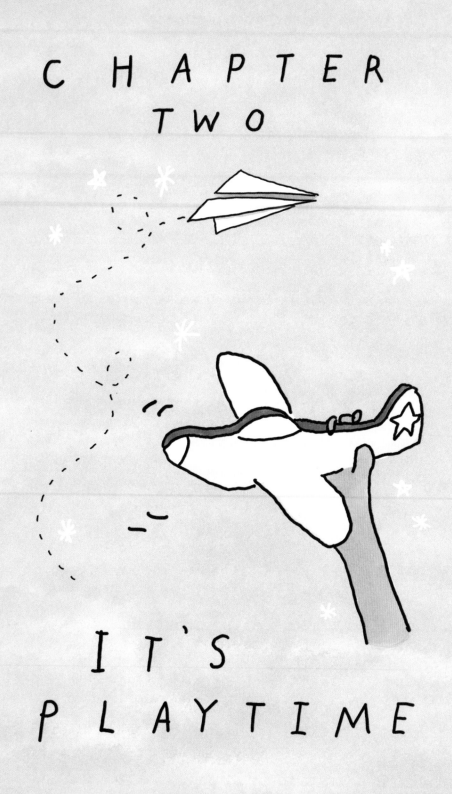

Time with children is refreshing, inspiring, and—I hate to admit this—exhausting. This is something adults said about me when I was a kid. The ten-year-old version of Brad had much more energy than I could ever know how to manufacture. Ten-year-old Brad never understood why all those old people were so tired. Yet here I am, writing about being exhausted. Maybe my exhaustion qualifies me as an official grownup.

You see, according to the kids I spoke with, being tired is one of our main ingredients. I asked them to describe grownups, and *tired* was one of the most repeated responses. I could see why they would think this. I've seen our social media posts. Generally, adults are either talking about a time we were exhausted, currently exhausted, or preparing for something we know will leave us exhausted. Exhaustion is just part of the deal when you become an adult.

It's a badge of honor: *I haven't slept in weeks.*

It's a generic response:

Grownup 1: *How are you?*

Grownup 2: *Busy! Tired! You?*

Exhaustion is also, if we're not careful, a default setting. We can get stuck in it. I have. I've been stuck in exhaustion for far longer than is healthy. In fact, part of what led me to begin this Listening Tour was total and complete exhaustion. I was burned out. This was an extra-crispy kind of burnout. A heavy travel schedule, years of overwork, and a refusal to admit I'd taken on way too much led to my inability to do anything. As I mentioned, sometimes I would just find myself lying on the floor.

I HAVEN'T SLEPT IN WEEKS!

MOM HASN'T SAID A COHERENT SENTENCE IN WEEKS.

My loving wife was the first to notice things were not okay. She urged me to see a counselor. The counselor urged me to slow down my schedule. My slowed-down schedule led me to have a little extra time. Having a little extra time led me to begin responding to teachers' requests that I visit their classrooms. Classroom visits led me to rediscovering the grownup I could become.

I'd become a tired grownup, and this only became more apparent as I spent more time in classrooms. I was surrounded by joy.

Joy takes energy. I was reminded just how energetic children can be. Children love to play around. They love fun. They don't need a reason. This came as no surprise. What did was the discovery of my own aversion to fun.

I thought I loved to have fun. I have always thought of myself as a very fun person. Before starting my Listening Tour, I'd thought I was still a very fun person. My time with children showed me otherwise. They would be laughing about something, and I would be the guy trying to calm everything down. I found great contrast in their ability to joke around and my inability to enjoy it. This wasn't because I didn't like them or didn't *want* to have fun. It's just that I wasn't there to have fun. I was there to become a better grownup! I wasn't there to play. The kids, though, seemed determined to undermine this very important quest of mine at every turn. There were moments of making faces at me, going way off topic, and sometimes responding to serious questions with animal noises. Yes, there were animal noises.

My first instinct was to think that the kids were trying to destroy my project. Actually, they were saving it and me from all the ways I'd grown old, serious, and seriously tired.

Of the top ingredients that make up adults, according to the students I spoke with, *exhaustion* was the fourth-most mentioned. Do you want to know what the top three were? Guess. You might think that kids said *wise* or *brave* or *successful* or *cool*. That'd be encouraging. *Wise, brave, successful,* and *cool* did come up, but mostly when students were describing the kind of grownup they wanted to be. No. The three words most used to describe the grown-ups in their lives were *big, busy,* and *boring.*

That's what they think of us.

On a few occasions, I asked children to draw what grownups look like. They'd grab a blank sheet of paper, begin using crayons, markers, or colored pencils, and unleash the most hideous things I could've ever imagined. This had little to do with their artistic ability and everything to do with each artist's intent. They would knowingly hold up their completed artwork in my direction with giant grins waiting to see my reaction. With just one simple prompt, the students had launched into a game of seeing who could create the grossest version of a grownup ever. Monstrous figures with exaggerated wrinkles. Raisin-faced people with hard edges around their eyes.

And that was just the beginning. They would gang up and begin adding to one another's drawings:

"Add a cell phone!" they'd say.

"Give it fangs!"

"Put lots of hair on their legs."

Yet when they were asked to draw someone specific, like a favorite grownup, their drawings were much more flattering. These featured parents and grandparents, neighbors and teachers. They would use cheerful colors and smiling faces. Clearly, not all grown-ups were disgusting monsters in their eyes. Still, their playful silliness revealed that somewhere inside them was a conflicted view of what it might mean to grow up. It was a conflict I felt along with them.

In her novel *Joy for Beginners*, author Erica Bauermeister has one of her characters say, "Adults need to have fun so children will want to grow up." Yet is it even possible to be a responsible grownup and not make adulthood look terrible? Students often described adults as people who work a lot, talk about work a lot, complain about work a lot, and miss things because of work a lot. They would share this in a matter-of-fact way, as if it were no surprise to anyone. They would also share this with a spirit of confusion, as if to say, *Why would a grownup choose to live this way?*

My instinct was, of course, to defend my own kind. Children couldn't possibly begin to grasp the weight we carry on our shoulders. We grownups have tons of responsibilities. We have family relationships and jobs to tend to. We wrestle with our existence and want our lives to have great meaning, but we also have to try to figure out how to fold a fitted sheet.

Folding a fitted sheet stands as the ultimate symbol of adulthood—it's impossible and will end in tears. So, who are these children to think they can judge me? I mean, *us* . . . to judge us? What do they know about fitted sheets?!

The giant wake-up call came during a video visit with a classroom in Wyoming. It was early in the morning of what was to be a full day for me. As the screen lit up, students began waving. From the get-go I could tell something was off. The students seemed more distracted than usual. They were pointing and laughing. No matter what I did to refocus the conversation, giggling continued. Finally, I stopped and asked. This was when they let me know about the poor internet connection. Apparently, the screen had been mostly frozen the entire time, leaving behind a ghost image of my head. When the internet connection returned, it appeared as though I had two heads.

The more unfunny I found this, the more hilarious it became to the students. One boy received big laughs by shouting with great concern in his voice, "That man is multiplying!"

Instead of playing along, I'm embarrassed to say that I got impatient. Ten-year-old me would've played along. Grownup me—not

so much. "Enough with the laughing!" Those are actual words I actually said. *Enough with the laughing*. That's something Gargamel would've said to the Smurfs. It's the kind of comment someone in authority says that only makes the situation worse—like an angry dad shouting to the backseat, "I'll turn this car around!" As soon as the words left my mouth, I realized I probably looked and sounded just like one of those monstrous drawings of what kids think a grownup is. Ten-year-old me would've been severely disappointed.

I liked to believe that I was a more enlightened grownup. After all, I was embarking on a project that celebrated children. As I listened to them talk about big, boring, busy grownups, I never once thought I fell into that category. Yet there I was. I literally asked some children to stop laughing. This woke me up to the many times I'd asked my own children to quiet down. They weren't being disrespectful or disruptive; they were just being kids. They were playing. All the pressures of being a new dad had clouded my ability to play. Even with this fun project of playfully listening to the hearts and minds of children, I'd found a way, against all odds, to make it not fun.

So is it possible to be a responsible adult and have fun? I am happy to report that the answer to this is a resounding yes. I discovered a better way to navigate the tensions between work and play, the secrets of which were found by watching teachers. Incredible, heroic teachers. While I'd assumed this project would put several inspiring children in my path, in equal measure I was introduced to grownups who truly showed me a better, brighter way of living. They weren't irresponsible, but they weren't afraid to play, either.

When Erica, an elementary teacher in the Midwest, invited me into her classroom, I immediately noticed a lack of chairs. She

seemed surprised by my reaction, but I was used to seeing desks and tables and classic classroom decor. Instead she had created and designed this learning environment as a space maximized for play. There were beanbags and exercise balls. You would think she was a physical education teacher, but this was the spot where students explored math and science and reading. This was where critical thinking and problem solving were taught. My first thought was that this setup had all the makings of a very bad idea. What about all the bouncing?

Where do you keep the bandages? How would the students sit still? I discovered that was actually the point. She explained to me how she wanted them to move around. She'd found that by allowing her students to explore and work together as a group, they came to life and engaged more fully with the material. They responded well to the freedom. "They have fun and don't realize we're all learning together," she said.

More than a dozen teachers told me about how they addressed fatigue in their classroom by instituting dance breaks throughout the school day. If they found that the students weren't responding well or felt the lessons weren't connecting, they would stop every-thing. Music would blast through a speaker, or a video would ap-pear on a screen. At this moment, everyone in class had to be on their feet doing their most ridiculous dance—even the teacher.

One art instructor in Utah helped me see how play can spark creativity. To help break her students of perfectionism and meticu-lously stressing over every mark they made, she would walk them through a certain exercise. I even got to take part in it. We were all given a blank sheet of paper and told to scribble on it. "No think-ing!" she said. "Just scribble! Have fun!"

When the time was up, we looked down at the erratic messes we'd all made. She then gleefully asked us to turn them into some-thing else. Now we were forced to completely reimagine our spontaneous scribbles, yet in doing so we made things we otherwise never would have. These messes were transformed into clouds and car exhaust.

What were once careless scribbles became beautiful horses and elaborate pompadours. By allowing the students to play, she'd unlocked a world of invention.

A history teacher in Alabama found a really playful way to have her students learn about the American Revolution. Instead of just lecturing the students or forcing them to watch a several-decades-old documentary, she had the kids pretend they were actually in that time period—except now they also had access to social media.

They were each given names of major figures in the American Revolution and asked to imagine what it was like to live in their shoes and tweet their lives. The students did not disappoint.

TWEET FROM GEORGE WASHINGTON:

So we riding in the boat to sneak up on these forts and Knox doing too much. Almost killed us his big tail making the boat tip. #BattleOfTrenton #CrossingTheDelaware #WeBoutDied

TWEET FROM SAM ADAMS TO GEORGE WASHINGTON:

@George do you got that info on that sugar act? #CantFixMyKool-Aid

TWEET FROM COLONIAL SOLDIER AT BATTLE OF SARATOGA:

It takes too long to load this musket. #ThisDoingTooMuch #AllForOneShot

TWEET FROM PAUL REVERE:

Man, I don't even feel like yelling so y'all just share this. #BritishAreComing #WeFinnaDie

TWEET FROM THOMAS JEFFERSON TO JOHN HANCOCK AT THE SECOND CONTINENTAL CONGRESS:

@Johnhancock dude, I asked you to sign the line, not the whole page. #Font1000 #CantFitMyNameNowhereNow

She told me the idea came out of her own passion for history. She'd found that if students could imagine these historical figures as real human beings and not just answers for a quiz, it unlocked curiosity and even compassion. They had to think about what it was really like to load a musket, worry about sugar prices, or be upset that someone had signed their name too large on the Declaration of Independence. They saw history as a real thing that happened with real people who had real emotions. By playing around, the students were placed in an active role of exploring the material alongside the teacher. They weren't sitting back and having the information fed to them. They were playfully engaged.

There was laughter and there was learning. That sparked an enthusiasm for learning more, which is precisely the hope of any teacher anywhere. Long after class was over, the students continued to think of things someone during that time might tweet. Some of the students even sought out additional reading to explore the personalities and the places beyond what was required. They were led into territory they never would've gone before had they not traveled playfully.

I grew up on a farm and remember my dad explaining the play of puppies as "practice." For puppies, being aggressive with one another is a way of being social. It's a way of play-acting real situations that might come up in the future for them. They're practicing. I grew up to find that my father's definition of *play* as "practice" was actually scientifically correct.

Stuart Brown, M.D., the founder of the National Institute of Play, has dedicated his life to researching what happens in our brains when we're having fun. Much of Dr. Brown's research in play wasn't done where you'd think—by watching children. Instead, his discoveries were found in extremely unplayful places—like in the lives of grownups. One of the most shocking findings? The absence of play was a major factor in predicting criminal behavior.

While it's commonly agreed that play helps humans develop socially, physically, and cognitively as children, the idea that it might continue to help us grow as adults is not exactly fully embraced. Yet when we are engaged in play, our brains light up. The neural connections that help us make decisions are the same connections that increase the more we play. It's been proven that playful activities like dancing or doing crossword puzzles, or dancing while doing crossword puzzles, can improve memory. But it goes even beyond that. When we play, we become more alive. Maybe because it's fun, we refuse to believe it's actually good for us.

Play is a very serious thing. We need it. When there isn't space for lightness, things can get far too heavy. When we don't have room to scribble and create, we can become rigid and even destructive. Better grownups are not too big, busy, or boring to play. They are playfully engaged with the world.

The great Fred Rogers once said, "Play is really the work of childhood." If Mister Rogers is right (and in my experience, he always is), I think play could also be the work of grownups. We'll have to make room in our schedules for it, though. That's one of the things I loved about the educators I met on my tour. They had made their work playful and built that spirit into their daily routines. As I visited classroom after classroom, I expected to meet teachers desperate for a break. I imagined my visits to their classroom would serve as a bit of downtime. Instead, I met deeply devoted educators who made learning—and growing up—look thrilling. They were right where they needed to be. I could see the joy on their faces. The students could, too.

After the incident with the two-headed image of me frozen on the classroom screen, everything changed. It made me realize how much I'd turned into a grumpy grownup who couldn't take a joke, and that was not who I wanted to be. I began taking my cues from the carefree students and their playfully engaged teachers. No longer would I approach the Listening Tour like a scientific researcher, but instead I'd be more like a friend who'd been invited to play in the sandbox.

By allowing the project to be more fun, and allowing myself to have fun in the process, I became more of myself. I was not big, busy, boring me. I became the curious, caring, fun person I'd always been but had allowed time to hide. We played. I listened. They shared. I learned.

There's another bit of important information about how kids see grownups that I need to share. For some of you it might be the most obvious, and for others, the most offensive. In addition to calling us big, busy, boring, and tired, kids don't think we can dance. They loved talking about this. When I say *loved*, I mean that it came up in nearly every classroom. It's one of their key points as to why grownups are boring.

It would go down like this: A student would speak up and share some story about their dad or grandma trying to do some dance.

There would be a sea of eye rolls. Then the whole class would begin laughing. By the twentieth mention of this, I decided to speak up.

"Not all grownups are bad dancers," I said confidently to a third grader, thus defending the honor of all adults everywhere.

"Oh really," said the girl. "What about you? Can you dance?"

"Well, no. I mean, I dance, but not very well."

The girl shot me a painfully unimpressed look.

"All I'm saying," I responded, "is there are plenty of grownups who can dance."

She continued to look unimpressed.

Now I know better. You cannot win an argument with a child without at least attempting to live as proof of it. If I wanted kids to know that you can grow up and do so joyfully, I would have to show them. We all do. We need better grownups to show future grownups what's possible. To do this, we must risk the embarrassment and dance.

But just as there can be a tendency to villainize grownups and portray us as simply big, busy, boring weirdos who can't dance, there can also be a tendency to idealize children and childhood. If we're not careful, we can misremember that time in our lives as simple. We forget that it's actually not easy to be little. As I visited classrooms, I began to remember how stressful it could be some days to make friends, follow all the rules, and remain seated in a chair. I remembered the struggles to fit in. I remembered the weight of wanting to make the grownups in my life proud. I remembered the deep feelings I had—but had yet to know how to even begin to articulate them.

Children have an ability to remain playful even with the barrage of pressures around them. Sometimes in the most serious moments, students would crack jokes. We could be in the midst of one of the silliest conversations, and a student would open up about deep sadness. One child would be telling me about unicorns and mermaids, only to switch gears and share how worried he was about something he'd heard on the news. I respect children's tenacious exuberance now more than ever. Amid all they are going through—the developments and the challenges—they still find delight daily. Certainly, we can do the same, even if it happens while folding a fitted sheet.

CHAPTER
THREE

ALL OVER
the MAP

When I found out we were having a child, the first thing I bought for him was a globe. There were plenty of much more useful items that should've been at the top of my list. Yet I immediately went out searching for a globe. Somehow his impending arrival gave me the impulse to buy him the entire world. This sounds ridiculous, I know. He'd clearly be too young to appreciate the sentiment, but that wasn't going to stop me. Not thinking clearly and determined to get that kid the world, or some physical representation of it, I bought a globe and placed it in a special spot in his nursery. It was an old globe. Several of the countries on it no longer existed. Much of it was inaccurate. Yet it's still our planet, and I wanted him to know about it.

At the time I didn't quite realize this, but I was tapping into something impressed on me by my fifth-grade teacher. There's much about fifth grade I can't recall. I remember only a fraction of it, and sadly it isn't the part where we learned about fractions. I think the teacher would be happy to know that a deeper lesson stuck with me. It was a simple spark that has only grown since.

We were preparing for a giant test on maps. This maps test had been hyped up for weeks. The teacher had distributed study guides. It was a very big deal, or so we were told. In the midst of this test preparation, a brave classmate boldly interrupted the teacher.

With an annoyed grumble, he initiated a classic teacher-student conversation. He posed a question, but it didn't seem like he really wanted a reply. None of us really expected one. The eight little words he spoke have been part of education discourse since the very first school bell rang. He raised his hand and said, "When are we ever going to use this?"

A classic, right?

The teacher did not explode. Her response wasn't gruff. I'm certain she was annoyed, but her reply didn't show it. She calmly reached up to pull down the retractable classroom map of the world. With her back to all of us, she turned to look at the map. She motioned toward it and said, "Look! This is where you live. This is your home. I'd think you'd want to know about it."

Now, I'd thought of my house as a home. I'd even thought of my classroom desk as a safe home. Yet I'd never thought about our planet as a home. The map was big and I occupied merely a teeny-

tiny pinpoint spot on it. That's it. Just a pocket-sized mouse tucked away safely with no intention of going beyond my little hole-in-the-wall.

I didn't have the courage to get up to go to a pencil sharpener, much less another part of the world. But that day, my idea of who I was on this planet and my place in it expanded. You don't forget days like that. Though I've forgotten many of the details of fifth grade, I have not forgotten that teacher or that moment. My sense of self and my perspective widened.

Great grownups have a habit of helping you do that.

Look! This is where you live. This is your home. I'd think you'd want to know about it.

In an effort to bring more playfulness into my classroom visits, I created a map. Not just any map, mind you. This was a treasure map. The idea was to have something I could share with students that would spark even more discussions. Often they would ask me questions, and while I wanted to be polite, I was there to listen, not speak. Because many of the students had watched videos I'd created or read things I'd written as part of their classes, they would often ask how I made things. Now, instead of giving an answer they might forget or misinterpret, I could provide them with a tool that might possibly help unlock their own making.

In an age of GPS and maps on our phones, we no longer get the satisfaction of unfolding a crunchy paper map and charting our course. Though students might be coming of age in a much different wayfinding era, the magic of having a treasure map in one's hands has never been lost. Each time I unrolled the map, eyes would light up. My favorite moments were in small classrooms where I could lay the map in the middle of the floor. The entire class—teacher included—would gather around to see. There'd be an electric hush as everyone moved in to get a view. I'd then ask, "So, where are you on the map?"

THE CLIFF of COMFORT
(POINT NOWHERE)
the STORY-FILLED SKY
OASIS
MEADOW of MEMORY
THE FOG of FEAR
THE COMMENTS
WONDER MOUNTAIN
THE FAR REACH
DIAMONDS OF HEART
THE MINES of HUSTLE
N
W
E
S
SCALE IN MILES
25 0 25 50
-BRAD
PER ASPERA AD ASTRA!

This is when things would get really interesting. The responses were always, quite literally, all over the map. Without hesitation, students shared the places they either were currently or had been recently. I loved how instinctively they'd pick up on the meaning behind different places. These were not physical locations, but internal ones: Inspiration Island, Doubt Valley, Meadow of Memory. All these are places one might find oneself at any given point in a day.

Originally, the map was created as a representation of places I'd visited. The treacherous waters of the Sea of Sharing have tossed me about for years, and I've practically kept a houseboat at the Sea of Insecurity. Many days have been spent in the sticky grasp of the Tar Pits of Approval. I've experienced success and seen a glimpse of the full beauty and grandeur of the journey as I stood atop Wonder Mountain. Yet I've also left the mountaintop to immediately wander lost and without aim through Doubt Valley. These were, in my mind, silly ways to depict very grownup feelings. The students, though, helped remind me that these were not silly, nor were they just grownup feelings. These were very human feelings.

I'll never forget a young girl named Amair and her brave response to the map. Surrounded by her fellow fourth graders, Amair leapt up. She pointed and repeatedly tapped on the Fog of Fear. "There," she said. "I been living right there." Her grandmother had passed away over the summer. She carried a deep sadness and was worried about losing other people she loved. There was no pause after she shared this. Her words were immediately received by caring classmates who hugged her and offered up thoughtful, encouraging words. She wasn't alone.

Comparison Canyon was a popular spot for many students. They instantly understood the pain of wishing you were someone else. One of my favorite moments with this little spot started when a fifth grader named Noah shared. Looking around at the other kids in his class, he commented on how his legs were shorter than theirs.

He felt as if he were looking over Comparison Canyon every single day because he wanted to be able to run as fast as they could. This is when the teacher spoke up: "You know, I was actually going to say that's where I am at, too." The students seemed stunned. This teacher went on to share how he looked around at other teachers in their school and wished he could be like them. As the teacher shared how he, too, understood the perils of comparison, you could see a powerful classroom bond forming. In the same way that I'd forgotten the complex emotions on this map were not just for grownups, many young people were surprised to find out that they were not just for kids, either.

COMPARISON
CANYON

The Comments section was originally included as a small, personal joke. Having done so much of my work on the internet, I've wrestled with online comments aplenty.

I depicted this section as a spot with very little life. Some nourishment can be found if you are brave enough. There's a cactus, but you do risk getting pricked by its needles. Beyond the not-so-subtle commentary on internet culture, many students found something beyond what I'd intended. A fifth grader named Jasmine said that she'd found herself in the Comments section and that she'd been trying to stop worrying about the things people said about her. That wasn't why she was in the Comments section of the map, though. She revealed that she was trying to add life to the Comments section. She knew the pain words could cause and she'd been trying to fill her school with better ones. I was blown away. This whole time I was thinking that I'd included the Comments section only as a joke about the internet. This young woman made me realize that it's an actual place we live in daily.

So much of where we are on the map is about choice—what we choose to do there and where we choose to go next. If at any time you find yourself

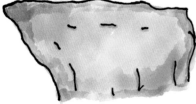

stuck somewhere like, say, the Tar Pits of Approval, you can choose to leave.

You can go climb mountains or explore valleys. You can also just stay in one spot. The Cliffs of Comfort are an option, but you do have to be aware of its other name: Point Nowhere. It's a spot where nothing happens. If you're looking to grow, all these places on the map must be momentary destinations. Choose wisely.

I was amazed at how much better kids understood this map than I did. As they spoke about the many locations they'd visited, I heard them articulate things I'd never quite put into words. This was especially clear when we talked about the Unexplored Territories. I'd marked them for a reason. Good cartographers are always interested in making their work more accurate, so I asked the students to help add to the map.

The students again amazed me. They added to the map with great imagination and even greater insight.

I discovered previously uncharted places like Guilt Gulch, Happiness Hollow, and Indecision Interstate. One classroom added a special spot they called the Good Place to Cry. Another classroom decided the map needed a dance floor. Students added problematic pirate ships and joyous jet skis to the seas. I was thrilled when one student drew a small circle and told everyone it was a portal to the other side of the map. He then flipped the map over and began to draw. The possibilities seemed endless.

This handmade map became the spark for some of the most meaningful discussions of the Listening Tour. Doodles of places I'd felt stuck in and scribbles of inner feelings I'd been traveling through had been filling my notebooks. Now, as I shared them, they inspired something. Students began not only adding to my map but also creating maps of their own. I was thrilled when a fourth-grade teacher named Mrs. Pagano sent me images of several maps her students had created. She made special note of one in particu-

lar. On this map, a student had built in a spot where all his favorite things would always be. He called it the Awesome Spot. In this spot, he'd placed video games, books, ice cream, and, much to her surprise, Mrs. Pagano herself.

Before this, he hadn't done anything that showed he especially liked his teacher. In fact, before this she wasn't sure they were connecting at all. He'd never taken much initiative to engage beyond what was asked of him. Now, here he was, drawing a map of the many places he'd been traveling and places he'd like to go. Plus, without even knowing she would see this map, he included her in the Awesome Spot. Mrs. Pagano realized just how much more deep exploration had been happening inside this young man than she'd ever thought. Even more so, she realized that she'd unwittingly been the exact grownup he needed to help him grow and explore.

As the tour went on, the map reached beyond classroom walls. Teachers began asking if they could use it with the rest of their schools' staff. School principals began pinning it up. Creative teams began using the map to discuss where they were in their process. One especially unforeseen use of the map came when a few different prison-rehabilitation programs discovered it. They found

the spirit of it to be a helpful way for men and women to express where they were and where they'd like to be as they reentered society. Through silly scribbles, I'd begun seeing people explore some serious things. I began carrying maps with me everywhere I went.

One spot on the map seemed to resonate with many grownups, though most students didn't gravitate toward it at all. Maybe kids weren't clear on what it was, or maybe they're just that wise. It was once one of my favorite spots, too: the Mines of Hustle.

Oftentimes people would ask me where I was on the map. I'd tell them I'd like to think I was in the Mines of Hustle. I tried to encourage people to move into these mines. This spot on the map was an expression of a lesson I'd been learning on the deep value of inner work. My thinking was that what we each need, and what the world at large needs, is more heart-led work.

Once, the person seated beside me on an airplane opened up about her struggles starting a new business. I handed her a map and told her how much we needed her in the mines, hustling not just for financial gain but also for diamonds of heart. There in the mines you can easily work for the wrong thing. She cut me off.

She explained that this new business *was* her heart. She had poured so much of herself into every part of this project. She was completely drained. The mine was empty. As she spoke, I could hear her exhaustion and it made me wonder if I'd been wrong about the mines. Maybe kids were wise not to gravitate toward this spot. In her voice I recognized the same dead-eyed burnout I'd experienced. The canaries had sung, and yet I'd continued the hustle to the point of illness. In my exhaustion I was trying to pull other people into the mines, too. She and I had both spent way too long in the mines. It was time to chart a different course.

I still visit the Mines of Hustle often, and I'd encourage you to do the same. But now I mine for a different kind of diamond. However, it's no longer the spot where I want to spend all my time. The

THE CAMPFIRE

place I encouraged my friend on the plane to go as soon as possible is the same place I'd discovered the wisdom of children: the Campfire. It is gathered around the warmth of the campfire where you can share the diamonds you've uncovered.

It is also there where you can pause and find nourishment in the warmth of community. It is where we share and feed both ourselves and each other.

Huddled around this map in classrooms, children helped me understand this. We have the ability to create bonfires of belonging wherever we go. We can also lose this gift if it isn't carefully tended to. Together, we can help remind one another of our place at the fire.

As someone trying to be a better grownup, my hope is for the people around me to see anew the world and their place in it. They belong and they are a spark to the fire. I now look at the globe I bought my son with different eyes. While I want to explore this planet with both my children, and while I want them to understand their significant place on Earth, there's much more that I long for them to know. I want them to know about the beauty of the world, but more so I want for them to know the beauty of themselves. Like my fifth-grade teacher pulling down the map, I want to pull down a diagram of their hearts:

Look! This is where you live. This is your home. I'd think you'd want to know about it.

I want to be the kind of grownup who hands out treasure maps to kids and goes digging for the good stuff with them. I want to help them explore the world around them and the hearts inside them. Because the thing about exploring within is that it helps in every place on the map you might land.

You will not only know about the world around you, but you'll also have the courage to change it, reshape it, and invite others into it.

If we can create safe spaces to be inner explorers of fears and doubts, mysteries and wonders, and explore those places together, we'll see a world with more heart. More listening. More sharing. More exploring. More inviting.

Handwritten and somewhat hidden in the lower right corner of the map is a Latin phrase: *Per aspera ad astra*, which translates roughly to "through difficulties to the stars." It's a little bread crumb—a tiny reminder that this is a process. There are no cheat codes to the good life. There is no shortcut to the stars—that Story-Filled Sky. It's a long journey. It'd be a lot easier to arrive at our destination in an instant, but were we to do so, we'd miss out on something vital. We need Doubt Valley and Curiosity Crossing, just as we need the wisdom learned from time spent there to be shared around any bonfires of belonging we might create. This is all a journey, and it's far better when not taken alone.

CHAPTER FOUR

HERE COME the JOY REBELS

When I was a child growing up in a small West Tennessee town, much of my window onto the rest of the world was books and television. Sometimes, in the midst of a steady stream of happy children's programming, an outside transmission would make its way onto the screen. Often it'd be tragic breaking news or a commercial for sponsoring children in another country. In my innocence I would inevitably be moved to want to take action. I'd have to do something—anything. The U.S. Forest Service used to run a series of ads that deeply affected me. They featured these raging fires that were started by some careless kids with matches. The advertisement would end with an animated bear named Smokey, who would say, "Only *you* can prevent forest fires." Seeing this, I took it upon myself to throw out every match in our house. I did not want to let that bear down.

It's a wonderful thing that as a child I didn't have access to any money beyond what was in my piggy bank. Aside from the fact that I would've purchased far more Pop-Tarts than any human should consume, I'd have thrown money at any person who appeared on-screen. Every single one of the ads about sponsoring children or donating to hospitals left me scrambling to find my parents. "WE HAVE TO HELP THEM!" I'd say. In these moments I was always baffled as to why my parents didn't seem to feel the same urgency I did.

Now, I had incredibly compassionate parents. My memories are filled with episodes of my mother and father going out of their way to help someone in need. Still, though, I can remember the confusion I felt when they didn't agree that we should sell our house and empty our bank accounts because I saw an upsetting commercial on television.

Some might call it naïveté, but that is being far too dismissive. A powerful, optimistic spirit is inherent to children and synonymous with childhood. In spite of any darkness that might cross their paths, kids are determined that things can be made bright. This isn't something fueled by anger or sadness. No, that would be *childish*. This is a joy-filled vision for how things should be. It's a rebellion against what currently is to create what could be. To be *childlike*—that's what we're after, because that is to carry with us the best of our youthful spirit. It is to be a rebel fueled by joy. It's a spirit I'd once known, forgotten, remembered, and then forgotten all over again.

Early in our marriage, my wife and I dreamed often of what we wanted for our lives. We had crystal-clear images in our minds of relationships that ours would be like and relationships that ours would not be like. Unwittingly, our entire lives we had both been concocting little lists in our minds of grownups we did and didn't want to emulate. Some grownups we'd seen had made maturity look miserable. Not us.

Oh, nay nay. We would be different.

We even put words to it. We declared our marriage and our lives to be a joyful rebellion. We wouldn't grow old and bitter. We would rebel against all that and with smiles on our wrinkled faces. We'd seen a few older folks allow life to beat them down and make them stodgy, fist-shaking "Get off my lawn" types. Not us. We would grow into vibrant, world-shaking "Welcome to our lawn" types. I don't know that this is necessarily a type, but it could be.

The two of us got jobs. We got a mortgage. We had kids. Still, we carried this joyful rebellion into adulthood, but with a bit of a limp. Time dampened our spirits. Discouragements came. My once soft and open heart hardened a bit. Troubling world news, which once would've caused a lump in my throat and a desire to act fast, now piled up. There was a twenty-four-hour news cycle of tragedy and a sea of people in need. The desire to do something was often still there, but it'd all become too overwhelming. Perhaps it was compassion fatigue or a creeping cynicism, or just a numbness to how big it all seemed, but I'd begun to lose my childlike sense of endless possibilities.

Even in the brightness of the Listening Tour, darkness could sometimes seep in. On one occasion, as I connected with a group of third graders via video call, the teacher informed me they were dealing with the sudden death of their classroom hamster. This was not what we had planned to discuss during our time together, but neither I nor the teacher—nor the hamster, for that matter—could have known the circumstances surrounding this visit. "Bingo" was a beloved fixture in Mrs. H's classroom and had been since the year before. A vote had been taken on naming the little ball of fur. Mrs. H thinks the winning name had a lot to do with the simple fact that the kids enjoyed saying "Bingo was his name-o." Meant to help the young students learn responsibility and to nurture a compassionate, caring classroom environment, today Bingo brought a new lesson into the room: death.

The typical topics of my classroom listening visits didn't seem appropriate on a day like this. I'd sent over some questions for the students to chew on beforehand, but now we were all sitting with a much larger question together: What does it mean to be alive in a world where there is death?

Mrs. H had given them the chance to help prepare a small memorial service to be held later in the day for the hamster. They were quick to share their ideas:

"I think he'd want us to draw him pictures," said one young girl, to the agreement of many fellow students. "We're also going to sing a song."

Another student quickly spoke up, "But we don't know what song yet."

As I listened in on their discussion, it was moving to see how much they didn't have figured out. They didn't know what the memorial service would be like. They didn't know what song would be sung. They didn't know how Bingo died or where he might be now. It was obvious, though, that the teacher had made it okay for them to be sad and okay for them to ask questions. They might not have all the answers, but they would walk through this together.

Over the course of a year and a half, I was finding that my classroom visits, and those very classrooms themselves, were not immune to unexpected interruptions. Sometimes these would come in the form of local weather or local tragedy. Sometimes interruptions came in the shape of global events. Lesson plans might have been prepared and agendas might have been set, but what happened that day would nearly always find its way into the schools, infiltrating the hallways and setting a tone. I'd found that educators are left daily to grapple with how to discuss current concerns while also, desperately, attempting to stay on schedule.

Throughout my tour of classrooms, I discovered amazing grownups who weren't afraid to go off-script or off-schedule. These were people who daily chose to walk alongside children even when it wasn't easy. Like Mrs. H, who pivoted her entire day to help students deal with the death of their hamster, these were grownups who served as guides through some of life's biggest challenges. They, of course, did this joyfully.

It takes a childlike spirit to be able to turn a problem into an opportunity. Puddles? That's a chance to make a splash. Budget cut? That's a chance to get creative. Death of classroom hamster? That's a chance to let every student know how much their lives matter.

It became such a regular occurrence to meet joyfully rebellious students and teachers that I created a little folder on my computer desktop to keep track of them. I named it "JOY REBELS" and filled it with inspiring stories of people I met along the way. That folder has served as a perfect remedy for those days when I inevitably forget that goodness is still possible. It's filled with stuff I need to remember . . .

. . . Kids like Evelyn. She started an initiative in her classroom called Less Garbage Every Day! At a time when most people I know are either simply ignoring climate change or in a panic about it, here was a seven-year-old trying to do something. She created handouts showing how we can reduce our waste and be smarter about our trash. After passing the handouts around her classroom, the teacher then helped Evelyn put them online. Now more people have access to something Evelyn made for just her class. Only seven years old and already aware that she can

joyfully rebel against how things are and
create what could be.

   . . . Classrooms like Mr. Nelson's and
his remarkably creative and compassionate fourth graders. They filled a jar with
names of people from throughout the
school—students, janitorial staff, teachers, and administrators. Each day they'd
draw a name and the entire class would do
something to brighten that person's day.
Some days they flooded that person with cards. Some days they
presented their celebrated person with a song. Every single day,
though, they found a way to make someone else's day.

   . . . Young people like Elijah Evans. He dreamed of throwing
a party for kids in foster care. It'd be a Christmas party, and he'd
make sure all those kids got exactly what they wanted. Why? Because he'd been a foster kid himself and knew what it was like not
to be fully known and celebrated. His project grew from throwing
just one party to taking shape as a bigger dream. Now he leads an
organization called No Use for Abuse. There are young people in

the world who've experienced pain no person should ever know. Instead of letting that sadness sit, Elijah is dancing through it and inviting all his friends into a party of possibility.

When Elijah told me about his Christmas parties, I flashed backward to being in fifth grade. Willingly dressed as an elf, I had wanted nothing more than to gather toys and help bring cheer to children I'd never meet. Now, many years removed, I'm much less likely to leap at the chance to wear a pointy hat and shoes. What happened? How could I have lost this joyfully rebellious spirit?

Part of what united my wife and me in making our marriage a joyful rebellion was the fact that we met as kids. It was at summer camp. The two of us would go on to work as counselors together at this exact same summer camp. When it came time to choose a place to get married, well . . . she suggested we get married at that camp. I couldn't have loved her or that decision more. One sunny June day, we were married in a lovely ceremony at the place that brought us together. Surrounded by family and friends, we exchanged our vows on the same wide-open field where we'd once played soccer, run relay races, and dreamed of what life might be like that far-away day when we were big and grown.

The two of us even went on to create our own summer camp. Just as camp had been an integral force in our lives, we set out to design a special kind of experience for kids. The focus was on social good and service learning. Junior high and high school students from across the country would gather to celebrate the many ways they could make a positive difference in the world. Sessions were led by young change makers who were leading projects in their communities. We got our hands dirty working together on things that addressed local and global needs. Meals were packed and shipped across oceans. Benches were built and set up in our town. Good was spread.

For five years, we witnessed hundreds of young people tackle issues like poverty, homelessness, hunger, racial divides, and challenges I'd never known existed. Through it all, I grew more and more aware of the power that young eyes have to see old problems

anew. Earnest love and deep joy were their fuel, and it seemed they had an endless supply of it. Yet I could sense my tank running dangerously low.

I had to regularly leave this planet of youthful optimism and return to the grownup world. On that planet, things were much different. There was a reigning cynicism. It was the kind of place where angry adults typed in ALL-CAPITAL LETTERS. There seemed to be a focus on everything wrong with the world. But I wanted to invite all these people to listen to kids. I'd found a world of young people who didn't just see problems but instead were seeking to be solutions.

Like Katie and Claire. These two sisters had been collecting new and used eyeglasses for an optometrist to distribute in Haiti. While

an older person might have debated back and forth the merits of whether to undertake such an endeavor, these girls had already collected hundreds of pairs of glasses. To them it was simple: Let's help people see better.

And Brent. He'd quietly been work-

ing to build the assisted-living center in
his town a better audiobook collection. I
know that doesn't sound too revolution-
ary, but to the folks living in that assisted-
living center, it was huge. To Brent, it was
special because his great-grandmother
lived there and loved to read. It was something
he could do for her.

In the midst of all the less-lovely grownup things swirling
around me, good was happening because of kids. Soup kitchens.
Donation closets. After-school tutoring. Kids all over the world believed that love could change everything, so they were out to fill the
world with it. Boxes and boxes of it.

Yet we couldn't run the camp forever. We simply couldn't af-
ford it. We'd tried to keep costs low enough so that as many young
people who wanted to be part of it could. Though it'd been successful in many wonderful ways, we didn't find enough support to keep
it going. The tension of running the program, balancing budgets,
managing logistics, and starting a family proved too much. We had
to step away, and it hurt.

Listening to young people in all their varied classrooms and
with all their varied experiences, I was rediscovering something
I'd thought I'd lost. That little spark inside me that once believed
anything was possible began to light up again.

I'd been stuck in the gap between the way things were and the
way things could be. I'd forgotten I had the ability to change that.

Part of growing up is discovering your power in the world.
When you see anyone, at any age, embrace their ability to make
a positive dent in the world around them, it's invigorating. Often
these are not grand gestures, but small acts of caring and daring
that have a direct impact on people. It's joyfully rebelling against
child*ish*ness to embrace a child*like*ness. It's trading selfishness for

THERE'S *the* WAY THINGS ARE.
THERE'S *the* WAY THINGS COULD BE.
THERE'S ALSO A *you*
AND THERE'S ALSO A *me*.

generosity, entitlement for compassion, fear for fascination, and anger for amazement.

We need people around us who can help us grow. As I'd see needs appear on my television screen as a child, it was my mother who helped me find ways to channel that compassion into our neighborhood. I'll never forget the day she suggested we collect toys to distribute at a local children's hospital. She'd heard many kids were stuck there with their families over the holidays. That suggestion nearly sent me doing cartwheels all over our house. The combination of collecting toys and doing something to help kids in need was more than my young heart could stand.

I was in fifth grade at the time and not yet too self-conscious to wear an elf costume. Dressed in green and red with a pointy hat and shoes to match, I joined my mom in delivering the toys. Friends from school and church had donated some, plus I'd gotten to make a few selections of my own to add to the mix.

We walked the toys in, walked back to our family car, and drove home.

Looking back, there wasn't much to it. It was a fairly simple little project, but it had a massive impact on me. I remember feeling like my mom and I had just done something wonderfully mischievous. It was like we'd broken some unspoken rule that said doing kind things was someone else's job. Dressed as an elf and looking in the rearview mirror while riding off in our family car—a.k.a. the getaway vehicle—I can distinctly remember thinking, *I have to do this again sometime.*

My circle of possibility had expanded. With my mother's help, I'd gone from caring about the one person in my circle—me—to inviting the other people in my circle—friends and family—to help people in a larger circle. I could look at the people and the world around me and dream up ways to make things brighter. No longer did I have to wait for someone on television to tell me what to do. I could find the need and do something about it myself. I'd just need to find an elf costume first.

In classrooms all over, I discovered millions of tiny revolutions happening daily. Within each conversation with any class, I'd discover some magnificent world-changing ideas packaged in what appeared to be, at first glance, very modest materials. There were small initiatives fueled by big love. There were little things outside teachers' job descriptions that were done to make their classrooms better places for humans to grow. It was a world of circles growing wider and wider.

As this project provided me with glimpses of goodness being lived out by so many different joy rebels, it had me wanting to design some Avengers-style situation. I wanted there to be an alarm that I could sound any time there was trouble in my life or in the world. I'd simply hit the button and they'd instantly all appear. Somehow, I thought, these heroic joy rebels all uniting in one place would make everything right again.

Thankfully, though, they're not all in one place. They are each in their individual towns and classrooms, simply shining where they're at in the universe. Just like how stars operate. Simply shining as they're made to, right where they are. For now, all I have is that little folder on my desktop. That JOY REBELS folder represents a whole lot of people living out a whole lot of love. It's reassuring to remember, when things get especially difficult, that millions of others are out there doing their part, right where they are.

Years ago Johann Wolfgang von Goethe said, "Everyone should sweep in front of his door, and every city quarter will be clean." A fifth grader named Sutton put it this way to me when she said, "Do your good things, and I'll do my good things, and there will be, like, so many good things." *Like, so many good things.*

JOY REBELS

Each generation rediscovers for themselves the magic of the world, but also the tragic nature of the world. How they choose to disregard this or engage with it has a lot to do with the grownups around them. Better grownups are joy rebels inviting us to grander views of ourselves and what we can do. They help everyone they come in contact with rise to new ideas of what's possible. In disagreements, in disasters, in deaths of hamsters, they still find ways to invite people into something beautiful.

I marveled at the caring calm of Mrs. H as she helped those young students come face-to-face with death. Yes, it was "just" a hamster and they were facing a full week ahead of test prep, but she knew this was not something to brush aside and ignore. Over the course of many classroom visits, I'd see this same wise calm as teachers navigated the loss of grandparents, beloved schoolteachers, and even students. Each time I'd see that they'd always find ways to use their embrace of sorrow to let every student know they were all vital fabric in the community quilt. I guess this is what it means to be alive in a world where there is death: to love.

I'd forgotten my power to joyfully rebel against what currently is to create what could be. Now I'm finding that I may not always have the words, but I can always find the love. I might not be dressing as an elf again anytime soon, but I am reinspired to be for kids what my mother was for me. I can be that helping hand attempting to creatively channel whatever kind spirit my children bring forth. It's my hope that my kids, any kids around me, and any former kids for that matter, all know that they can make a difference and know that I will be by their side to help. There is, after all, the way things are, the way things could be, and, most of all, us. There's us. Knowing this will lead to endless possibilities and to many good things.

Like, so many good things.

CHAPTER FIVE

· TINY masterpieces ·

Martin Sheen can be very rude in conversations. Once, he and I were both at a large conference celebrating young people making a difference. I was attempting to act like this was normal. While backstage, we began chatting about films and books. I'd loved him in the television show *The West Wing* and especially loved his work with director Terrence Malick in the film *Badlands*. Every part of me was geeking out as he began running down a list of books Malick had encouraged him to read that had changed his life. Then Martin abruptly walked away.

He'd found someone much more interesting to speak with. As I watched him rush toward a pregnant woman, my face fully displayed the betrayal I felt. I stood awkwardly off to the side like someone at a party who'd been abandoned by their date.

He threw out question after question:

"When are you due?"

"What's the name?"

"How are you feeling?"

Martin then began cheering for this woman and her soon-to-be-born child. He lifted his hands in the air and said with a giant grin, "This is fantastic!" It was as if he'd never met someone expecting. Both he and the pregnant woman were laughing, and at this point, I was, too. Here was someone cheering enthusiastically for a child who wasn't his and, in fact, belonged to a total stranger. As she walked away, Martin returned to our conversation, still glowing.

"Sorry," he said. "I always stop for babies."

There's a way of seeing children that I've found in the best of grownups. It is the way of seeing children as hope. It is seeing children as a fraction of our population but all of our future. It is a way of hearing a screaming newborn on an airplane and not being annoyed but feeling extreme gratitude—okay, so maybe that's a stretch. Still, there's something wonderful that happens when we see children as wonder and as hope. We find reasons to stop, to cheer, and to live with renewed purpose. The Indian poet Rabindranath Tagore

once wrote, "Every child comes with the message that God is not yet discouraged of man." Every child is another chance.

The flip side to this is something I'd not really thought about until spending so much time with children. It's the way children view adults. Yes, their drawings and conversations about grown-ups were sometimes silly and grotesque. But when the grownups they loved and trusted walked into the room, they didn't just see another person. They saw an image of hope. It seems, when we're doing life correctly, both children and adults begin to see hope in one another.

At the same time I was discovering the power of hope, though, I was discovering that the limits of my listening project were beginning to discourage me. Specifically, it was the limit of time. I started to realize just how little of it I was spending with each classroom. The teachers and parents and other grownup guides were with these students all the time. I was just a guy miles away who'd appear only briefly and then disappear. Like Santa, except I didn't really bring gifts. I mean, sometimes they got maps. Oh man, I'm realizing what a terrible Santa I am.

Often students would open up about considerable challenges in their lives, like the separation of their parents or the loss of loved ones. In these moments I'd especially feel the limits. For one thing, I was dedicated to listening, not speaking. For another, I was not a licensed counselor or anyone who could actually walk with them through these difficulties.

After conversations like this, I'd always check in with the teachers to make sure they had heard what the student brought up. Every single time, without fail, they were

already well aware, already walking through it with them. Already being great grownups. Of course they were.

I think, in large part, I'd begun feeling these limitations because the project was inviting me to grow. I was stretching beyond my old form of hiding. Through creating videos and writing stories, I'd concocted safe ways to connect with the world at a distance. Hiding behind cameras and scripts had become my life: a way to affect the world without any of the dangers that come with real human interaction. Even these virtual classroom visits had become a way to connect with teachers and their students without having to really do the messy work of walking alongside them. A desire grew in me to do more than just show up and then disappear.

The great instigator for this next step came when I got a big, uncomfortable invitation. Big, uncomfortable invitations are the kind I immediately say no to. They're so big and so unreasonable that there's simply no way I should accept them. Then I get a good night's rest and find myself, inevitably, talking it over with my wife, who makes me realize it's exactly something I should accept. This big, uncomfortable invitation was to be part of an event at the

Guggenheim, one of the world's greatest and most renowned art museums.

I was being asked to speak—something I'd not done in front of an audience on a stage in a very long time. I'd only recently gotten the strength to get up off my office floor and start talking to a counselor.

My classroom listening project was, at this point, in its early stages. I'd grown comfortable enough speaking in that setting, but my words were brief and spoken mostly to children. This would be to a room full of fancy grownups, and that room would be in one of the world's most iconic museums. I wanted to survive it, but I also wanted to find a way to make it special. Though there probably wasn't a whole lot I could do in that department besides smuggle a painting out under my shirt. That would make it memorable! So would getting arrested.

Looking in my office at all the children's art I'd accumulated over my classroom visits, a thought occurred: *What if I smuggled art into a museum?*

A plan was hatched. I messaged my network of classrooms with a strange request. Last time, I'd asked them if I could just listen to them. This time, I wondered if they might send me some art. I let them know it was for a fun project. My plan? Smuggle all their artworks into the Guggenheim.

I wanted to blast out into the world what children had already shown me so much of: hope.

So I asked students to send me art depicting what hope looks like. More than five hundred submissions came in. My inbox and mailbox were giant piles of hope. There were rainbows and sun-

shine. Drawings of families and teachers. Things I'd already heard kids speak about were now represented on construction paper with crayon. This gave me something tangible to put out into the world that shouted the wild optimism of children. Likewise, now they could all forever say their artwork had been shown at the Guggenheim. Never too early to build your résumé.

The other limiting thing about the Listening Tour had been the solitude. Though I was connecting with people, it was for the most part online or through very quick travel. I was alone for the majority of the time. For someone who was healing from a long stretch of overwork with too many demands and too many people, the break from giant crowds had been healthy. Now, though, I was in need of more connection. I needed a friend. More specifically, I needed a partner in crime. My great joy rebel of a wife, Kristi, was exactly the person I needed.

We arranged for our parents to watch the kids. We explained the reasons for travel only in vague details. The reverse art heist would be, um, hard to explain. Plus, this way, they could have deniability should anything go awry. Information, however, began to leak online. By "information began to leak," I mean I carelessly dropped too many bread crumbs about smuggling children's art into one of the world's finest art museums. By "bread crumbs," I mean that I posted specifically about it on Twitter. One quick pro tip for any future reverse art thieves out there: Don't do that. This, of course, happened to catch the attention of someone at the helm of the Guggenheim's social media accounts. Thankfully, they seized the opportunity to have a bit of fun. I think the event organizers had probably tipped them off already anyway. They played along and even slipped me little clues about great places inside where someone could show "rogue art they brought in from kids should they be foolish enough to do so." Challenge accepted.

Now Kristi and I were like kids playing, and the world was playing along with us. We packed up all the students' works and boarded a plane, our suitcases and hearts full of hope and maybe even a little mischief.

You can't help feeling a sweeping sense of awe as you enter the Guggenheim. The slanting spiral ramp creates a feeling of endless possibility. Architect Frank Lloyd Wright was ninety-one years old when he died, six months before the building's opening, proving that one can remain full of childlike imagination and innovation plus have buckets of grownup wisdom and know-how up until the very end. Wright once admitted to "stealing" the idea from the shell of a snail. I think the snails of the world would forgive him.

While experiencing the wonder of the setting, we also experienced the absurd realization that we had just smuggled five hundred pieces of art into a museum. I had a small bag stuffed with as much art as we could fit. Our coats and pants were lined with art. The crunching sounds we made as we walked had to have tipped people off that we were up to something. Perhaps they just assumed our clothes were heavily starched. All the packing and sneaking and crunching would be worth it, though. We were hope

smugglers. We would make certain all five hundred pieces were displayed.

The fun work began. Kristi took the camera and began to film me holding up different pieces. These created grand images we could send back to kids.

They'd see their work proudly displayed among masterpieces of modern art. Then my arms got tired. This was the point I realized what a terrible bandit I was. Bandits don't complain about their arms getting tired. But it was dazzling to see their work brighten up the place. The kids had used whatever materials were at hand to bring to life what was in their hearts. Watercolors, markers, crayons, and glitter were popular media. Try as we might to be discreet, the glitter did leave a trail. Kind of how hope leaves a trail, too.

To get people to interact with the art, we started making new friends. The two of us began letting museumgoers hold these pieces of hope and hear the stories of these kids. In the same way that people analyze masterworks by artists officially displayed on a wall, some took the same approach to these children's drawings: "One thing that's really clear from this artwork is love." "Fiercely innocent, messy, and bright. I love it!" "It reminds me of how much I like watching my kids do art." "I used to make stuff like this when I was a kid. And I wish I still did."

Fiercely innocent, messy, and bright. Yep, these works of art had the power to light up the entire building. People smiled. People cried. Some people were confused. Hope does that to people.

When asked to create artwork depicting hope, the students took fascinating directions. Some had created their pieces together. Entire classrooms had gathered and collaboratively marked up a giant poster. A few sent videos in which the kids sang songs, while others performed skits about people who gave them hope. Much of the art was brightly colored and featured things that brought smiles to the kids' faces, like animals and shapes and smiley faces.

Many illustrated hope as a superhero. One young girl, though, really took it to the next level. She created her own superhero. Aubrey painted an alter ego named Doodle Girl whose sidekick is No. 2, a pencil. Her mission, and she'd definitely chosen to accept it, is

to inspire creativity and defeat her archnemesis, Dr. E. Raser. This evil baddie is always on a mission to destroy and be negative. Doodle Girl wants none of that! Aubrey's brain made me so happy. The fact that she had these dreams in her head and shared them thrilled me. As I hung up her Doodle Girl artwork in the Guggenheim, I wished that she'd hang on to this hopeful spirit and imagination throughout her whole life.

So many children depicted hope as loved ones. They covered their art with family members and friends. Holding hands or sharing meals, people united and belonging—all glimpses of what a more hope-filled world might look like.

Though it took some creative problem solving, we found a way to display every single piece of the art we brought to the Guggenheim. Some of the larger pieces didn't lend themselves to travel, so we had them printed on postcards, which we passed out or left lying around the museum. And there continued to be a steady stream of late submissions even after we arrived at the Guggenheim. So Kristi loaded them onto a tablet that we passed

around so people could see them. I wanted every child's contribution to be seen and celebrated. Most of all, I wanted to spread the hope they were sending.

We didn't get kicked out or arrested. Our kids and their grandparents didn't have to come bail us out. Instead, the good people in charge at the Guggenheim loved the spirit of the project so much that they set up a special wall. They allowed us to officially put up several pieces, and as I did, I was beside myself with joy. For these selections, I chose some entries from a few third graders who had really blown me away. Other children had drawn families, friends, and loved ones, but these figures were drawn especially close together, hugging and smiling. I'd noticed this but hadn't realized the backstory. Then I read the accompanying letter. These pieces of art were from Mrs. Lee's classroom, where many of her students had only just moved to the United States. These refugee families, originally from Iraq and other countries, were now figuring out new lives at this new school in a new country.

Like all the other students, they'd been asked to draw a vision of what hope looked like. They presented an overwhelming focus on safety, warmth, and community. These students understood hope as a future with everyone they loved being held close, safe and happy together.

One piece from a student totally caught me off guard. We'd gone through all the art many times, and I was certain I'd seen everything, but this one found a way to slip past me. Maybe it was so I'd see it at just the right time. It was a smaller drawing, very simply done. My wife handed it to me and said, "You've got to read this."

A young boy had written five simple words:

"Hope is where we are."

I thought about him sitting in his class and being asked that question: *What do you think hope looks like?* I wondered how long it took him to land on that supremely wise statement. I wondered who'd walked alongside him to help him understand that. However he came to know it, I'm grateful he shared it. It's what I needed to hear. Maybe you do, too.

There I was, trying to smuggle hope into a museum. I thought we were doing something really daring and rebellious. Yet here was a reminder that hope isn't something you have to sneak around or pirate in. Hope isn't something you pack up and lug around. Hope is wherever you are, right under your feet. Wherever you go. Wherever you are today, hope is right there, too. Just as we look at children and see hope, they can look at you and see hope standing in front of them. Because hope is right where you are. You are sneaking hope into every place you go. Just by being you. You're a masterpiece of hope.

With that boy's five little words, my shoulders—and my soul—relaxed. Doubt had crept into my project as I wondered if my listening and my little encouragements to children were adding any hope to the world. I'd wanted so badly to do more. I desperately wanted to spread and smuggle their hope everywhere, but I'd forgotten something very important. Hope was already wherever I went.

My friend Larry is a retired minister. At age seventy-seven, he carries with him years of wisdom from his time spent trying to love and lead people. Quietly he still does just that, loves and leads. One day he told me something that really got my attention. He said he had boxes and boxes of children's artwork.

"Why?" I asked him.

"Well, because years ago I vowed always to keep anything given to me by a child," he said.

"Anything?"

"Anything."

His boxes and boxes contained scribbled renderings of him in crayon, unidentifiable blasts of color on construction paper, and many macaroni necklaces. Of course, he'd kept them. Some of them were presented to him as children's prayers, their tangible hopes of something better given to a man they felt had direct access to God. Seeing their generous, loving spirits made him feel that they knew more about their creator than he did at times. He would grow emotional as he recounted stories of children who were walking through grief and yet drawing him such dazzling depictions of hurt mixed with hope—rainbows of resilience pointing the way to the joy they'd found in spite of seemingly impossible circumstances.

He kept anything given to him by a child because, in his eyes, it was the purest gift he might ever receive. It was children's way of letting him know they saw him as hope. The gifts were spotless expressions of deep love. They were not given with expectations of awards or acclaim. They were given eagerly and audaciously so the children could let their friend Larry know that he meant something to them. Anytime they might feel like one of God's little mess-ups, they need only remember the way Mr. Larry had looked upon them as his eyes and smile assured them that they were nothing short of

glorious. These were tiny masterpieces. Both the art and the artists.

Haley Curfman is a second-grade teacher in Blackwell, Oklahoma, who also understands this very well. Her classroom is a cheerful place where students fall in love with learning and have fun in the process. Never one to keep the status quo, she's always on the lookout for ways to make the classroom more exciting. This led her to discover something she'd seen a few other people do in different settings, which was to get a plain white dress and cover it with paint. So one day, she brought in a plain white dress to her class and told the students to decorate it for her. She then promised to wear it. Students were allowed to put any message they wanted on the dress. The looks on her student's faces when they saw her not only appreciating their work but also actually wearing it told her she'd have to make it an annual tradition. For the past few years, she's done just that.

I wonder if maybe that's how we let the people around us know they're irreplaceable. We seek out any and all ways to show them how they mark and brighten our lives. We place their expressions of love on our refrigerators and office walls. We look them in the eyes and promise them it will be a gift we'll remember forever. Or maybe, like Haley, we physically wear their work to show just how much a part of them is a part of us.

After the Guggenheim show, we settled back into our routine at home and paused to hug our children a little tighter each day. The great hope smuggle continued to replay in our minds, though. One day, after several months had passed, I received a link to a video on YouTube. Mrs. Lee's class had done a TEDx Talk, and it was all about having their art smuggled into the Guggenheim. I melted at hearing the story from their point of view. Taking turns at the microphones, these students proved they had a lot of hope to share with all of us. They shared how the project sparked conversations with their parents.

In the speech, one of the students says, "Many of our parents are refugees. We started to have conversations with our parents to find out what *hope* meant to them. They shared about faith, they shared about their kids, and they shared about their beliefs. We started to recognize that we were hope in their eyes." In response to the art piece that stated, "Hope is where we are," they added some profound words. One of the students stood at the microphone and said, "Hope is *where* we are, because of *who* we are."

Hope must be who we are. It means being able to recognize it in others and celebrate it. Should a child draw something for you, it doesn't take smuggling it into the Guggenheim to let them know you loved it. Hanging it on your refrigerator will do. Even more simply, your presence can do it, too. It's just pausing from what you're doing and celebrating the hope you see in them. I guess what I'm saying is . . . Martin Sheen was right. We should stop for all babies. Constantly be wise enough to stop and celebrate hope, even if you're talking to me.

part two

FORGETTING

Though frightening for her father,
it was beautiful to see
a graceful, smiling girl
gliding from tree to tree.

Quiet places were discovered
where she could fly outside.
Her father would watch from below
with feelings of great pride.

But as the girl grew older,
the pressure, it grew, too.

And slowly something happened—
less and less, she flew.

So in tiny pieces,
little by little, and day by day,

the whole problem of floating
simply floated away.

By the end of grade school,
she didn't float at all.

By the end of junior high,
it was just a dream; that's all.

High school and college ended.
The daughter moved away.
She took a job and grew up
as they'd all hoped she'd do one day.

No one could recall
or say quite what had happened.
Was the floating they'd seen real
or something they'd all imagined?

But every now and then,
something she saw or felt or heard
would make her heart skip a beat—
like looking up to see a bird.

She'd think to herself, "Dear girl,
something must be wrong with you."

Yet, somewhere not too distant,
her father felt it, too.

CHAPTER SIX

SIX WORDS from FRED

"I think they forgot how hard homework is," said Zachary. Some of his classmates laughed, but his eyes had a resolve that told me he was serious. Fifth grade can be tough, and Zachary was right in the midst of an especially challenging stretch. He opened up about how tough the school year had been so far. He was feeling that his parents, and even his teacher who was in the room as he said these words, didn't understand the difficulties of maneuvering everyday life as a fifth grader. There might've been a time when they had been in similar shoes and felt these struggles. However, that time had passed, they'd forgotten it, and Zachary wasn't going to take it.

A few of his classmates chimed in with "Yeah!" and "Mmm-hmm!" It was like being part of a lively town hall or a spirited church service. His words about homework had struck a nerve. The students began talking about all the ways the grownups around them had forgotten the difficulties of being a kid. They spoke of feeling misunderstood and stretched thin. I wanted to laugh as they mentioned the stresses of doing small household chores. Cleaning their rooms and putting away laundry didn't seem to merit the sort of passionate frustration they were showing. I wanted to tell them about what they had to look forward to, with income taxes and health insurance and having to constantly unsubscribe from email lists. Yet as they spoke, I felt distant memories of similar feelings I'd once had.

I was in elementary school the first time I heard rap duo DJ Jazzy Jeff and the Fresh Prince. It was a music video for their song "Parents Just Don't Understand."* It's funny to think now, but I sat there as an elementary school kid in the Deep South. My circumstances could not have been further from those of these two West Philadelphia rappers. Yet as I listened to that song I remember nodding my head and thinking, *These guys get me.*

Now, I was finding that somehow I'd become the kind of person DJ Jazzy Jeff and the Fresh Prince rapped about. One boy named Benny said, "I can't believe my grandma was ever a kid." From what I gathered, he and his siblings lived with this grandmother. She apparently expected a lot from them. "She's all the time giving us work to do and getting on me about grades." When I suggested to him that she likely did all these things out of love, he knit his

---

*This song was written by Jeffrey Townes, Peter Brian Harris, and Willard C. Smith. Another fun fact: DJ Jazzy Jeff's real name is Jeffrey Allen Townes, and the Fresh Prince, who sometimes goes by the name Will Smith, once lived with his auntie and uncle in Bel Air, and has saved humanity from aliens more than once.

eyebrows. The perplexed expression informed me that I was now a grownup who did not understand.

One thing I've found to be true is that all great grownups are simply trying to communicate love. Sometimes this love is spoken by teaching responsibility or nurturing growth through challenges. Sometimes with words. Sometimes with hugs. Often, though, this love doesn't translate, as different generations can seem to speak different languages. For these jumbled attempts at getting love to reach its mark, it takes a patient and persistent messenger.

When we're children, we communicate like musicians who are still learning to play their instruments. Imagine the supremely talented Louis Armstrong with a song fully formed inside him, yet with no way of bringing it out into the world. We hit the wrong notes and play in the wrong key. Sometimes we can't even find our trumpet.

Surrounded by kids, I began to remember this feeling well. I'd been a kid who had cheered and complained. I'd whined and I'd thrown fits. Sometimes I actually did these things at the appropriate times.

We might've forgotten it, but we all once spoke the language of children fluently. We were all once small and fumbled to find the proper ways of expressing the many feelings we felt.

Sometimes it might sound like we grownups now speak a different language than we once did, but children are not that different from us. Children are communicators of love, too. All words and actions—whether they come from children or from grownups—

FRED ROGERS
(TV host, teacher, great grownup)

are either a statement of love or a request for love. This was true
of all conversations I had in classrooms and, I'm finding, true of all
conversations any of us will ever have.

"Love is at the root of everything, all learning, all relationships—
love or the lack of it." Like most of the elemental things I've learned
in my life, this was taught to me by Fred Rogers. *Mister Rogers'
Neighborhood* was a staple of my earliest childhood.

For years I thought he was speaking directly to me. I've since
learned that was part of his gift, as millions of other children felt
the exact same way. By seeing how he proceeded through life in our
daily television neighborhood visits, I gained a better understanding of how I fit locally in my neighborhood—just by being me. As
I've grown, I've come to understand it has equal bearing on how I
move in the world as a global neighbor.

Mister Rogers was teaching me when I was 3 years old and will
likely continue to be teaching me should I live to be 103 years old.
Even with having "outgrown" his television show many years ago,
I've stayed an active admirer and student of his work by seeking
out anything he ever did. From speeches to television appearances,
I've devoured it all.

One day I happened upon something surprising. I found out that Fred wrote a chapter in a medical book titled *Duane's Ophthalmology*. Yes, Mister Rogers wrote a chapter in a giant book for ophthalmologists. So I hunted it down on eBay. When the massive thing arrived in the mail, I immediately sought out Fred's words. The chapter title? "Physical and Psychological Preparation of Children for Anesthesia and Surgery." Never had I imagined I'd read something like this on purpose.

What could he possibly say that these doctors hadn't already learned in medical school? What would he add to this very technical book? A workday for Mister Rogers was singing little songs and playing with puppets. What could this host of a preschool television show have to share with real-life doctors and surgeons?

His chapter begins with this line:

"You were a child once, too."

You were a child once, too. This small statement might seem glaringly obvious at first reading. It's something we all know. Of course, we were all once children. Yet, reading it again, I was struck by his invitation to remember. It seemed to me an audaciously simple thing to write in a book aimed at medical professionals, or in any book at all.

Could those doctors working on young children serve them better by remembering that they, too, were once children? By recalling the feelings and emotions of being small and unprotected, would they perform their medical work in a kinder, gentler way? Could this be the key to being not just a better ophthalmologist but also a better grownup?

Sure, they have training. Certainly, they have expertise. Somehow, though, this straightforward appeal to reflect on the child they once were, could—in his estimation—be transformative. It suggests placing yourself in these children's shoes. These are smaller shoes, yet similar to ones you might've worn not too long ago. It proposes having the imagination to recall what it might've felt like to be in those smaller shoes and the needs, fears, and longings that come with them.

Maybe that's part of why Mister Rogers began every episode of his television show putting on sneakers. He would walk into the room singing his song, change into a sweater, take off his dress shoes, and put on a pair of casual sneakers. Repeatedly putting on different shoes, modeling for us what it's like to place ourselves in a different perspective. Every time he spoke he was appealing to us all to see everything in a new way. For ophthalmologists, that's exactly what they're working to do: Help others see. With his exquisite humility, that's exactly what all Fred's work did, too.

Just as these doctors would be standing before young patients, medical instruments in hand, we now stand in our respective stations of life. We are the grownups in the room. There are needs around us and there is work to be done. Reflecting on the children we once were could give us great clarity in how we serve the children who now surround us—and the grownups, too. We, after all, were once young, too.

Thinking this way would cause us to rethink everything. We

would reimagine how communities are built and how classrooms are structured. We would take great effort to create nourishing stories for screens of all types. We would elevate how we work with and for children in all fields. We'd begin to see every person of any age with more compassionate eyes, realizing that they, like us, were once young, vulnerable, and in need of loving care.

One of the earliest projects my wife and I did together explored this idea. We wanted to see what might happen if we allowed adults to relive childhood memories. Kristi posted a few words online asking friends to share some of their most beloved life moments. Then, in a bit of playful fun, using cardboard, glue, yarn, and markers, we made it our job to re-create those moments as best we could. Time travel on a budget.

Sasha: "When I was a little girl, I loved visiting my nana. She owns a chicken farm and I used to love helping her unload chickens when the Tyson truck brought them in. There was a big fan near the windows to keep them cool, so when we'd unload the pallets, tons of baby chicks would fly everywhere."

Kim: "One of my favorite memories is my first day of kinder-garten. I wore a blue-and-white-striped dress and had a purple backpack. My hair was in a side ponytail and I remember thinking the bus was huge. I was so excited."

Chuck: "When I was really little, I used to take all the Tupper-ware out of my mom's kitchen cabinet and crawl inside to play. I loved just sitting in there by myself."

Colton: "When I was four, I climbed inside a laundry basket and rode it down the stairs like a roller coaster. The ride was awesome . . . the ending was terrible."

There was laughing. There were tears. Cheap crafting materials, which they likely played with as kids, had somehow come together to bring them to a moment from long ago. With what was—at first glance—a very silly photo project, they entered into these cardboard reconstructions with a profound reverence. Each person stood reunited with a magical moment from their childhood.

That moment might have gone, but the children in them were very much still alive. We could always tell by their glowing faces.

In describing memory, Oscar Wilde said it's the "diary that we all carry about with us." I think some of our pages are always easily accessible. These are light and cheery places we can visit at any time. These are the dog-eared pages that take us to a rose-tinted ideal of what our childhood was or could've been. These are the memories we readily share as anecdotes about growing up and the ones we'd love to have re-created for us out of cardboard and string so we could relive them and play again.

WE ARE WALKING DIARIES.

Of course, these diaries we carry around also contain heavy and tragic memories. Be it the loss of a loved one or a traumatic event of any kind, these pages contain shock, strain, and stress. Unpleasant to visit as they may be, they are significant entries we shouldn't erase. These take us to a turning point where life shifted. Sometimes these are the parts where we say we had to "grow up." They are chapters in our story we might not like to reread, but we know very well the ripple of impact they've had on every word and sentence of our lives since.

All of us have even more memories beyond the ones we can easily bring to mind. I don't suggest or recommend living in the past. This is, after all, a book about growing up, which should involve moving forward. I do believe, though, in the importance of remembering and understanding how our pasts have helped bring us into our present, wherever that may be.

We get knocked around and tossed about. The demands of daily life thrust us forward in time. Like we're on a fast-moving treadmill and stubbornly refusing to slow down, we keep going. Along the way, we pick up nicks and bruises but keep moving forward anyway. This is, after all, what is demanded of us. Forward motion is what we do. We pick ourselves up and we get on with life.

Over time, though, the dings and scrapes accumulate. We find ourselves forgetting where that bruise came from or why that scar is there. We can't quite remember where we picked up that desperate need for approval. Some of the larger scars we, of course, can recall with vivid detail. The rest, the blurry little hurts, those have added up through the years to simply become part of who we are, even though they hold us back from becoming who we're meant to become.

After my time at the Guggenheim, I found myself having more energy. I'd continued seeing a counselor, who started noticing the same thing. I was definitely more upbeat than I'd been when this journey had started. She'd been the one who'd originally encouraged me to slow down my schedule. Counseling and self-care had been completely new concepts to me, but thanks to them I was now beginning to feel a considerable fog lifting. Gradually I'd begun

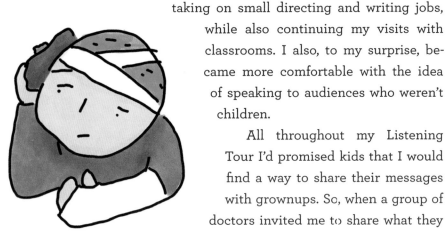

taking on small directing and writing jobs, while also continuing my visits with classrooms. I also, to my surprise, became more comfortable with the idea of speaking to audiences who weren't children.

All throughout my Listening Tour I'd promised kids that I would find a way to share their messages with grownups. So, when a group of doctors invited me to share what they could learn from children, I jumped at the chance. While questioning what I should say, I immediately remembered the words of Mister Rogers. I thought of his gentle call to those ophthalmologists so many years ago. Instead of trying to impress them with surgical experience I didn't have, I'd share with them his plain admonition to look back and focus on this truth: "You were once a child, too."

My confidence in sharing these simple words began to wane as I looked out at the audience from backstage. The auditorium seats were filled with brilliant men and women who had dedicated their lives to the medical profession. I was a writer and director of silly things for kids. It was too late for a rewrite, so I would have to proceed with what I'd prepared. Though my voice shook, I shared kids' stories. I shared their hopes. I shared Fred's invitation to remember. As I did, I began to realize just how much I believed in its importance deep in my bones. A passion I'd lost had been rediscovered and, in spite of all my nervousness, the message resonated.

I wrote down the words of one man who spoke with me afterward because I knew I would need to always remember them. He was the kind of well-dressed doctor type that I'd always assumed had all the answers. Had he and I passed each other on the street or in an elevator, I would have thought we'd have little in common. Yet there I stood, washing my hands in the men's room, and there he stood with tears in his eyes.

He described to me a day when his network of hospitals had asked everyone to bring in a childhood photo. It was supposed to be a lighthearted workplace get-to-know-you sort of thing, but became way more. His mother had sent him an old photograph of himself from when he was five years old. It had been taken in a department store and he was wearing a winter coat.

Of course there were many obvious differences between the adult standing in the bathroom and the child in the photo. He'd gotten taller. He'd lost hair. Also, at age five he didn't have a mustache. The profound moment for him came when he looked closely at the photo and into his own eyes. They were the same eyes he still had now, except with one major difference: Now they weren't as open. Through tears, he kept repeating the question, "Where'd that kid go? Where'd that kid go?"

I wrote his question down and think of it often. Anytime I find myself with someone vastly different from me, I can always go back to that question. Somewhere inside them is still a child. We're all united by the fact that we've been children. Maybe what separates us is that some of us have forgotten this.

There's something else Mister Rogers said: "The child is in me still and sometimes not so still."

While we're on the topic of Mister Rogers, may I share something with you? Throughout this project, many inexplicable things happened, and this one took my breath away. I'd begun sharing this message of becoming a better grownup by becoming more like children—to doctors, educators, parents, and anyone else who would listen. One day I received a message from the Fred Rogers Center. Dramatic pause. Zoom in to see Brad screaming. Zoom out to an image of the world in which you can hear Brad screaming.

The Fred Rogers Center was holding an event for people who work in children's media to discuss how the spirit of Fred's work could continue in the world today. For this event they were asking me to share a few words. You could've powered an entire city with the boost I got in that moment.

THE CHILD IS IN ME STILL and SOMETIMES NOT SO STILL. —FRED ROGERS

The Fred Rogers Center is in Latrobe, Pennsylvania, where Fred grew up. So, in a way, it's the original Mister Rogers' neighborhood. The Fred Rogers Center is tucked away in a quiet part of town, and every corner holds some historic piece of his story. I was allowed to spend time in the archives, where I devoured letters, speeches, and scripts. I got to meet Joanne Rogers, Fred's wife of nearly fifty-one years. Best of all, she hugged me and told me I was special. I'm fairly certain I flew.

I struggled with how to share something at this event that might match the honor I felt or the respect I held for his work. That is, until I remembered Fred's very own words in the book for ophthalmologists. Just as I'd shared them before with the medical community, I'd do the same for these children's-media professionals. It seemed fitting to continue the tradition and make the anchoring point of my talk those little words: "You were a child once, too."

While the response was kind, I never could have predicted what happened next. Afterward, a woman approached me and introduced herself. Her name was Hedda Sharapan, and she'd worked on *Mister Rogers' Neighborhood* from the very beginning. I recognized her immediately but tried with all my might to play it cool.

"I have to tell you something," she said with a stunned look.

She explained how she'd started working for Fred shortly after graduating from college. Her work on the television show evolved over time and often took many forms. As the show grew, Hedda's role transformed, and she became an irreplaceable part of the team. Sometimes she'd work with curriculum, sometimes she'd work in research, and sometimes she'd assist in writing. Once, during a particularly busy season, she was tasked with helping research a chapter Fred had been asked to write. It was going to be included in a book for ophthalmologists—the same book, *Duane's Ophthalmology*, that I'd discovered all those years ago and had just spoken about from the stage.

Hedda grew emotional as she told me about how she wrote this chapter and then passed it on to Fred for his review.

"His standards were so high. His work was so meaningful that whenever I presented anything to him, I really wanted it to be the very best," she told me.

Oftentimes she'd send him things and preemptively write at the top "for your revision." Fred didn't like that word, as it seemed negative, so she began putting "for your elevation." This made him laugh, but at the same time gave a perfect description of what she felt he did for her. He elevated Hedda and her work to an entirely new level. So from then on, when Fred would make notes on her writing, he would sign it, "—your E.O.," which stood for "your elevator operator."

"Fred was an incredible appreciator," she told me. There were times when she felt insecure about what she brought to the small team. Once, after a meeting in which she felt like she'd added nothing, Fred sent over some papers along with a note saying, "Thanks, Hedda. You're a great synthesizer." Having just left a meeting in which she'd shared very little, he'd just validated her silence. He knew that she was serving in her own way and was a vital part of that room.

"I thought, you know, it's okay that I'm not the person on staff who is offering the creative ideas. I am someone who has another role here. It's a different role, and it's one that's appreciated."

When Fred returned the chapter she'd written for the ophthalmologists, he'd made suggestions throughout, as he often did. But his editing on this particular piece of writing stuck with her, and would now forever stick with me as well. As she looked at the notes, she saw that Fred had done something astonishing. He'd nixed a substantial portion of the beginning and replaced those lengthy opening passages with those six words: "You were a child once, too."

Hedda and I stood together in stunned silence.

In a book meant for ophthalmologists, I'd found words that shaped me into something better, that had helped me grow, and that I had shared with a room full of people I'd never met. In that room was a woman who heard a reminder of words from a mentor in a talk delivered by a stranger, and just had to let me know. Somehow, extraordinarily, those words "You were a child once, too" had found their way across space and time to connect us both. The elevator operator was still at work.

"He helped me grow," she said. "Thank you for helping me remember."

There is a word in Ghana, *sankofa*, that means to move forward by going backward. Some translate it to mean "go back and get it." The word is represented in West African culture as a bird. The bird's feet are firmly planted forward, but its head is turned to look back. In the mouth of the bird is an egg, something precious it has retrieved to carry into the future.

It is a brave bird that brings past treasures into our present and future.

Now and again, we could all benefit from a visit into our pasts. Light could be shed on where our insecurities came from. Where our anger began. Where our joy was lost. Bringing this understanding of who we are into the present can help shape the way we embrace everything. Like this bird bringing something of value from the past into the future, our doing so could allow us to move forward by going backward.

I am grateful for children. However, I am especially grateful for the children I encountered on the Listening Tour. They helped me remember. Through their laughter and their complaints, through their insights and their critiques, these students took me back to a time when I was new. I received the painful and wonderful gift of being able to travel backward in time. This has allowed me to approach all conversations, all relationships, and, especially now, fatherhood—from a place of deep love.

When wondering what in the world we could do for the children around us, better grownups remember. Better grownups remember they were once children, too. Knowing this, they spend their lives as elevator operators, simply lifting the people in their midst to the places they need to be. Time passes. Technology shifts. Trends change. Yet there are basic things all people always need. Maybe tending to those unchanging things can help us change everything.

Once childhood is remembered, the real work becomes not forgetting.

CHAPTER SEVEN

BE who YOU NEEDED

Fred Rogers used to do something wonderful when speaking to live audiences. He would close by inviting everyone in the room to spend one minute silently reflecting on specific individuals who had helped them become who they needed to be. The people who, as he said, "smiled you into smiling, people who have talked you into talking, sung you into singing, loved you into loving." In a masterful move, he'd take the spotlight that'd been placed on him and have it somehow shine on everybody else.

There's a clip of Fred doing this at an awards show, which I'd seen years ago. As it was passed around online, I originally assumed he said it only that one time. However, as I dove through hundreds of his speeches while at the archives of the Fred Rogers Center, I found it was something he did repeatedly. This wasn't because he didn't have anything else to share or say. The audiences were diverse—Hollywood stars, heads of state, educators, or migrant workers—and he'd have important personal messages for each. Though large portions of his speeches might change, this silent, reflective minute remained a key part of his message to adults. It was his steady reminder that no matter who we are, we all matter to each other.

One minute might not seem like a long time, but it does when you're seated with hundreds of people in complete silence. Some people would cry. Some people would laugh uncomfortably or try to ignore the exercise altogether. But something in the sincerity and the resounding truthfulness of this message would leave the room in a quiet awe. Even in video clips of these speeches you can feel the power of remembrance as each room basks in the glow of this rare reflective gratitude. At the conclusion of his minute, the gentle and thoughtful Fred would then say, "Whomever you've been thinking about, imagine how grateful they must be that you remember them when you think of your own becoming."

Imagine how grateful they must be...

Children begin understanding this at an early age. In our conversations, kids were eager to share stories of wonderful grownups. They weren't always complaining about things they wished grownups would do or say differently. In the same way parents or aunts or uncles might beam about the kids in their lives, many kids would swell with great pride when talking about the grownups in theirs.

This was from a fourth grader: "I love my mom, because she does so much for my sisters and me. She's working two shifts and making sure we have everything we need." I don't know if this student could've really told me what a shift is or what "working two shifts" means. Sure, she might not know all the particulars, but I do think she fully understands that her mother is working hard. Most important, she understands her mother is working hard and doing so out of love. I don't know if she'd ever said this to her mother, but I'm certain her mother would've been proud to hear what her daughter was saying about her.

Other students shared stories about grownups they knew who were taking classes at night to get college degrees. They spoke openly about parents who were starting and running their own businesses. These students seemed to understand the risks and the sacrifices of career and raising a family. There seemed to be many real-world struggles these kids knew and grasped in ways that I definitely didn't until I was much older.

These young people seemed to be on a mission with the grownups in their lives. There was a sense that they were all wrapped up in it together. Like members of a team, they were a small part of a larger whole. In every classroom there'd be a handful of students who'd share about the people they lived with, and I'd end my time with them hoping that one day my children or other kids in my life might speak of our family in that way. Sometimes these conversations could be heartbreaking, but more often than not they were inspiring.

The more I heard kids talk about the people they admired, the more I wanted these kids to tell those actual people. Sure, I enjoyed their stories. But I couldn't stop wondering what sort of good might happen if they spoke this appreciation to their loved ones directly. With that idea in mind, I decided to try something.

I began presenting kids with this fill-in-the-blank:

I am _____ because you were _____. It's pretty simple. Like, you might say: I am CONFIDENT IN WHO I AM because you were ALWAYS ENCOURAGING ME. Or I am ON THE SOCCER TEAM

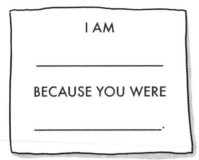

because you were THE ONE WHO TOLD ME I COULD DO IT. I am WHO I AM because you were IN MY CORNER. It's a statement directly affirming that our identities now—who we are at this very moment—are tied up in and somehow the result of the person someone else was for us. It is one thing inspiring something else. It is the origin of our becoming who we were meant to be.

I began sharing these little printouts with students I visited. The instructions were easy: Fill in the blanks and share it with the influential person in your life. This was something that would have to happen beyond my time with the students. Because of this, I had no assurance that kids would actually do it. I was approaching that dangerous territory of being a guy who'd shown up only to give them homework. My goal when starting out on this mission was just to listen. But from what I'd been hearing, these kids had so much to say, and I wasn't the only grownup who needed to hear it.

A fifth-grade teacher sent me an image of a scrappy little printout. It said, "I am GOING TO COLLEGE ONE DAY because you were MY EXAMPLE." The teacher then filled me in on the backstory. "He took this home to his brother," she wrote. "He's just started college this semester, which is a big deal for their family. Their father is in prison, so this is a commitment that both of these boys are forging a new path."

Not surprisingly, many teachers had students present notes to them.

"I am GOING TO BE ON THE HONOR ROLL because you were PATIENT WITH ME," wrote one student. She placed it on her teacher's desk without signing it. It's tough to surprise a teacher, though. They know the hearts—and the handwriting—of every person in the room. Though this teacher immediately knew who the surprise note was from, she was surprised by the message on it. "She and I have had a long year," wrote the teacher. "I was blown away by her confidence and pride in her academic work. I'm going to treasure this message from her. I was already proud of this girl, but it means so much to know that she's proud of herself, too."

As elementary school students began appreciating the people in their lives, other students at their schools began joining in the fun. Classrooms of older kids began using the idea. Teachers and administrators joined in the gratitude. When I began sharing a few of the stories and posted the prompt online, even more gratitude came pouring in.

I am ALIVE because YOU DIDN'T GIVE UP ON ME.

I am FEARLESS because you were BRAVE.

I am SERVING CHILDREN NOW because you were
CARING FOR ME THEN.

The internet became a patchwork quilt of "I am _____ because you were _____" responses. It became a way for people from all walks of life to acknowledge mentors, coaches, guides, and friends. Selfishly, it became a way for me to hide from a discouraging news cycle and focus on hope. These were reminders that one human can completely alter the course of another's life. I marveled at the honesty and beauty of each one. With every new story, I was granted a perspective that allowed me to transcend whatever else was happening in the world that day. There might've been dark or discouraging headlines, but I was getting a daily text crawl showing me the truer, quieter news happening all around.

An email with a photo of an entire college campus holding up "I am _____ because you were _____" signs found its way to my inbox. This school in Searcy, Arkansas—Harding University— urged its entire student population to pause and recognize someone who'd made their lives better. They did it. The photo made my heart do cartwheels. Thousands of students filled with gratitude held signs representing people who believed in them. I thought that surely there'd be no topping that moment. But it was just the beginning, as I'd find out several months later.

Little did I know that in that photo was a man named Steve Shaner. When he was presented with the question, he knew exactly whom he wanted to celebrate. The first person who came to mind for him was the same person who'd always come to mind for him: his eighth-grade teacher, Mrs. Dorothy Fisch.

One of five children, Steve was never the best student. When he was an eighth grader in Middletown, Rhode Island, he'd already been in and out of ten different schools. His family had moved around quite a bit, and with each move, Steve got a little further behind in school. This had an effect not only on his academic and social life but also his confidence.

Mrs. Fisch's classroom was unlike any other place he'd been before. It was an English class, and he'd never considered himself much of a reader. This class should've been hard for him, but instead it turned out to be one of his favorite places in the world. Steve remembered how Mrs. Fisch read aloud to her students, something that brought books to life. For the first time,  everything clicked. School suddenly made sense. Much later in life, he'd be diagnosed with a few learning disorders. He didn't yet understand how differently he processed information from how his classmates did. One of those things he'd later discover is that he is an auditory learner. Mrs. Fisch's reading aloud was exactly what he needed. Neither he nor she had any clue just how much.

In Mrs. Fisch's class, Steve even found himself being excited about homework. One of the assignments for her class was to create a magazine. The project required writing articles, creating advertisements, designing a cover, and even pitching it to the entire class. Having never done these things in his life, Steve found himself coming alive. "I got into that assignment like Ralphie writing a theme letter to Santa Claus." It was his first A+.

Then came the real kicker. On his first A+ assignment, Mrs. Fisch added a note with the grade. She wrote, "You should go into journalism or advertising. You would be really good at that!" So that's what Steve did.

As he sat in the audience with the university students, Steve's mind went back to Mrs. Fisch. He began to go through the grand timeline of his life. Her guiding light and gentle revelation led him down a path. With just a few words on a class assignment, she'd launched him into a lifetime of work he loved. He'd gone on to get a degree in mass communications, work in television, radio, and photography, and even become part owner of a small community newspaper. His colorful career was tailor-made for his gifts. His life had been more than that scrappy, unpolished, unconfident eighth grader ever dreamed it could be before her note.

He was now a professor with students of his own. As he looked out at all the university students holding up their "I am _____ because you were _____" signs and heard them commit to sharing it with the person who'd believed in them, he panicked. It'd been forty-nine years since he'd last seen her. She was the teacher who'd changed his life. He'd never told her. Was she still alive? Was he too late?

Steve had no leads. He didn't know where she was living or *if* she was living. A brief internet search turned up nothing. He tried

everything he knew, but Mrs. Fisch was nowhere to be found. He'd
waited too long. His expression of gratitude would now be just a
cautionary tale. He'd share this story with the university students
as a grand reminder to never forget to thank the people who helped
shape you. Don't wait until it's too late.

Then he found her. In a roundabout way, Steve came across
the Facebook profile of a woman named Dorothy Fisch. There was
no way to be certain, but he felt confident enough to send her a
message. Now instead of searching for her, he was searching for
words—the right words. He had to explain who he was and why he
wanted to reach out. Realizing this could be interpreted as creepy,
he began second-guessing his entire mission. One doesn't often
get dispatches out of the blue from people you haven't seen in five
decades. Even so, Steve took a risk and sent the message. Then . . .
he waited.

Nothing. Weeks passed and there was no response. This was
either not the right Mrs. Fisch or he'd totally freaked her out or—
and this is what he was holding out hope for—she just wasn't active
on Facebook. Gradually going from professor to detective, Steve
noticed her profile picture had a handful of likes. So he crafted a
message to her friends.

Then it happened.

Steve got a response from one of Dorothy's friends who went
by the name Cookie. She'd later reveal that she'd gone to great
lengths to make sure he wasn't up to any trouble. "We checked you
out real good," she told him. You see, just as Steve loved Mrs. Fisch,
well, so did her friends.

So what had Mrs. Dorothy Fisch been up to? She'd continued to
teach school after Steve had last seen her. In total, she'd taught for
twenty-eight years, reading aloud countless books and impacting
even more students. Since retiring from the classroom, Dorothy
had been living in Delaware. There she spent a large amount of

her retirement as the children's librarian at the local public library, where she led the story hour.

Though more than a thousand miles separated them, Steve made arrangements to thank Mrs. Fisch in person. On that day, Mrs. Fisch walked into the library, as she'd done many times before. That day, though, was different. That day, as she entered, there was an anticipation and a swell of joy. That day, in a building she loved, filled with books and stories and dreams, Dorothy was greeted by someone she hadn't seen in many years and had no reason to think she'd see again. Someone who'd never forgotten her words. Her presence in the life of a young person forty-nine years ago had boomeranged right back to her.

Through hugs and tears, Steve took a moment to step back. As he did, he asked, "Are you really Dorothy Fisch, my eighth-grade English teacher from forty-nine years ago?"

"Apparently I am," she said. The two laughed.

He'd brought along two of his grandchildren, who looked on as stories were swapped about life and time and the wonder of it all. Cookie, of course, was there, too. Dorothy's local newspaper even showed up to document the occasion.

As they talked, Dorothy and Steve pieced something together. She'd have been only twenty-three or twenty-four years old when he was in her class. This was very early in her teaching career, a time when most educators or anyone

starting a new job feels at their most inadequate. Even so, here they were. She'd done something right.

Steve has a wall in his office that's covered with photos of students who've gone through his classes. Some he stays in contact with. Some he might not hear from for forty-nine years. He's started calling it the "Fisch effect." Each of those photos represents a person he might never have met had she not entered his life just when he needed her.

He told Dorothy about the wall of photos, about his career, and about the trajectory of his life. He looked at her and said: "I am who I am because you, Mrs. Dorothy Fisch, encouraged me." There were tears. There was celebrating. This was a thank-you forty-nine years in the making.

My wife, Kristi, and I have a sign in our workshop that says, "BE WHO YOU NEEDED WHEN YOU WERE YOUNGER." This has been a guiding principle for us and an animating force in our work for many years. It's influenced everything she and I have ever done. None of it—service-learning camps, *Kid President*, the curriculum we've created for classrooms, or the Listening Tour—none of it would exist had we not asked, "How can we be who we needed when we were younger?"

I think going to this place in your mind unlocks memories. It also, I believe, unlocks purpose. When you reflect on how you can be who you needed when you were younger, bubbling up inside you will be pleasant and painful reminders of the support you had or the support wish you had. You'll realize you now have the power to be the grownup you maybe forgot you could be.

It seems better grownups are the kind of people who live with great purpose. They operate out of gratitude for the kind of support they had when they were younger and work to fill that role for everyone around them now. It's as if they're operating as living thank-you notes, with every interaction becoming a way to

express gratitude to the person who helped them grow. Better grownups also operate out of a desire to provide others with the kind of support they perhaps didn't have. Their lives become a joyful rebellion against what they didn't have so that others will have it. Most of the better grownups I've met are living as some mixture of both. Always, though, understanding they have the ability to make a lasting impact.

I met a male educator who purposely serves at a school because he didn't have any positive male influences in his life. He's being what he needed when he was younger. I met another educator who survived a traumatic childhood and now serves as a school counselor. She's being what she needed when she was younger. We can all find great purpose when we remember our inner child's great needs.

One day a student stopped me in my tracks. She asked me who I put down on my "I am _____ because you were _____" sheet. Funny, I'd been asking people all over the world to fill these out and hadn't really been asked about my own. I'd been content to retreat into the beauty of everyone else's messages. Who would I put? I drew a blank.

My mind went to my parents and grandparents. I thought of neighbors and relatives and family friends. All of them were vital in shaping me, but this Listening Tour was clearly the result of a grownup I needed when I was younger. I hadn't put words to it, but then it hit me. This was all my fourth-grade teacher's fault.

In fourth grade, I was a chronic doodler. Some students would finish tests early because they were good students. I, on the other hand, finished my tests early so that I could draw on the back. Any blank space on any paper was my canvas. These would be epic drawings of birds and self-invented cartoon characters. They wouldn't just be for decoration; these were adventurous stories that I just had to get out of me. My thinking was that the teacher would never see these or pay them any attention, because it was the back of the test. She'd be too occupied to notice. Except she noticed.

Mrs. Perkins began giving me little assignments to draw things for the class. She talked about them in front of everyone. The older students at our school had just started a newspaper. She encouraged me to submit some comics to them. To my surprise, they accepted them. Everyone else who wrote for the paper was in junior high or high school, and here were these little comics from an elementary school student. I couldn't believe she saw value in my little doodles—or in me, for that matter. For some reason she believed in me. She even told me, "You're very creative. You could do anything you want."

It was her encouragement that led me to package up some of my drawings and stories. She said I should send them to Walt Disney. I didn't have the heart to tell her that Walt Disney was dead. Even if he weren't, it was silly to think that anything I had to share with the world would matter to anyone. I was just a pale farm boy from a small town who liked to doodle. There's nothing sensational about that. But her words—"You're very creative. You could do anything you want."—played and replayed in my mind.

One day I finally got the courage to send the Walt Disney Company several of my drawings. I even got an old tape recorder and used it to record a message for them. There was a note in there, too, about who I was and what my dreams were. I think I may have even put a few pieces of candy in, just in case that might push them over the edge. I found an address for the company and mailed them all my hopes and dreams.

Weeks passed and I forgot all about it. Then one day I came home from school and checked the mail as usual. Walking from our gravel driveway to the house, I thought I saw mouse ears on one of the return addresses. My eyes jumped out of my head. I dashed down the rest of our driveway, practically hovering over the rocks. When I made it to the door, I erupted into the house with an announcement: "EVERYONE! I GOT A LETTER FROM WALT DISNEY!"

"Walt Disney is dead," said my brother.

"No, no, no! This is from people who work there! They wrote to me! They got the package I sent them!" Already I was thinking about how I'd have to move out of the house to be closer to them. I began wondering what we'd do about school. My teacher had been very supportive of my creative endeavors, and I was sure she'd be an advocate for me there.

My clumsy hands pulled the letter from the envelope and I began to read aloud:

Dear Mr. Montague, _____ ➜
THAT'S ME!

We received the package you sent us . . . _____ ➜
THEY GOT MY MAIL!

Words, words, words, words . . . _____ ➜
GROWNUP WORDS I DON'T KNOW YET!

The letter seemed to go on and on. I didn't understand or comprehend all of it. I was pretty young at the time. I just knew it was a letter from PEOPLE WHO MADE STUFF LIKE MICKEY MOUSE. My insides were throwing a party. Confetti cannons were going off. Balloons were lifting from my heart and up into my head. Then I read the last line:

For legal reasons we cannot accept submissions from outside sources. We do hope you understand.

Then it was signed by somebody I didn't know. My hands continued to grip the letter. The look on my mom's face confused me. It was one of those sympathy expressions that moms give when they're preparing for you to let all your emotions out. She was about to console me when I interrupted with a cheer: "They wrote me back!"

Obviously, I hadn't grasped that it was basically a cease and desist order from sending them unsolicited materials. To me, it was a giant wink from the universe that I was on the right track. I existed! This giant company knew I existed! It would be many years before I fully realized what the letter meant or actually said. As part of this official form letter there was, however, one small personal element. In the bottom right corner in red marker, someone simply wrote: "You made our day! Thanks for sharing your voice."

I don't who wrote that or why. Maybe it was inspired by the candy I'd included in the package. It could've been that they were moved by the fact that a young kid had the courage to mail something out. Maybe they understood the power a few encouraging words can have on someone. Either way, it was the same exact message Mrs. Perkins had been trying to get through to me: My voice mattered. I mattered.

Many years removed from that time in my life, I now found myself in a classroom. This time as a grownup being asked by a fourth grader why I was doing what I was doing. My answer: I am trying to let children know they matter because you, Mrs. Perkins, were persistent in telling me I mattered.

I think often of Mister Rogers and his invitation to reflect and remember those people who "loved us into being." The reason my wife and I have the words "BE WHO YOU NEEDED WHEN YOU WERE YOUNGER" hung up in our workspace is the same reason he asked people to sit and reflect for one golden, silent minute. We matter to each other. We need each other. We are poorer in strength and spirit when we forget this.

Who we are to each other helps shape all of us. We are all the products of the cumulative caring of many people. There's a phrase people often use: *made my day*. We will say, "Aww! You made my day!" or "You said I made your day and that just made my day!" Somehow we have all the materials needed to make each other's days. If we were to take time and really think about this, we'd go wild making days for each other. We'd craft them and design them to be truly unforgettable days. But we forget. At least, I forget. I'm trying to remember more.

On the day they met up, nearly fifty years after he'd been in her classroom, Steve had one last request of Mrs. Fisch. He asked if she'd mind reading a story to his grandchildren. She found a book, they sat at her feet, and she read. Just as she'd done so long ago for their grandfather, she read. With her gentle voice, which had altered their grandfather's life, she read. Steve's grand-children listened intently, and when the story ended, Mrs. Fisch closed the book and placed it back on the shelf. With that, all had come full circle.

CHAPTER EIGHT

THE BETTER QUESTION

? ? ?

The questions most grownups asked me when I was a child were "How old are you?" and "What grade are you in?" Kids do not ask questions like this. Smaller children might introduce themselves by declaring how old they are: "I'm three!" But this is usually just a starting place for the real things they want to talk about. From there, they typically begin to elaborate on favorite animals, cherished toys, or uncomfortable observations they've recently had about human anatomy.

The more time I spent with elementary school students, the more I wanted my interactions with all people to be like them. Those kids asked great questions. They were consistently present. They were supercurious. They weren't interested in basic-introduction, résumé-type stuff. There was no concern for knowing my age or my job. Nope. With a freewheeling, childlike wonder, they would ask me if I had any pets. They'd ask if I'd read their favorite book. They wanted to know if I played video games. Once a student asked me if I'd ever seen a potato explode. I'd never been asked that in my life. They asked the kinds of things that led to far more interesting places than just sharing how many birthdays I'd had.

If only we adults were more childlike in our conversations. We tend to focus on things like what people do and where they live. We gather basic stats and then, generally, move along. Never do we get to the really good stuff, like "Have you ever seen a potato

EXPLODING POTATO
(ARTIST'S RENDERING)

explode?" There is, however, one awesome grownup who showed me what a childlike curiosity and a thoughtful conversation could look like, and it came from a source that surprised me: a Supreme Court justice.

It all happened when my young brother-in-law and I were invited to a fancy dinner. This would require us to dress up. Not a big deal for Robby, as he could simply wear the suit he wore when filming *Kid President*. For myself, I'd have to make sure my suit still fit. Stress eating had complicated my wardrobe options. That wasn't the only thing making me anxious. I'd grown to despise events like this because they felt like entering a grade-school lunchroom all over again. You try to walk with purpose while also not being exactly sure which direction you're going. Your eyes scan the entire room, hoping to spot someone you know. Should you be unable to find someone you know, you take a risk and ask someone if you can sit with them. Having chosen your fate, you now have to try to not get any food on your nice clothes.

Then come the questions.

Just as grownups often have stock questions we ask of children (e.g., "How old are you?"), there are scripted questions we have reserved for fellow grownups. These are things like "How are you?" and "How about this weather?" These are harmless, friendly, introductory sorts of things. The question that strikes terror in my heart, though, is the perennial, "So, what do you do?"

I fantasize about just straight-up lying. I want to say, "My name is Chad and I am a . . . doctor." Nobody would ask another question. *Oh, we get it. You're a doctor.* I think about how impressed they'd all feel to be seated at a table with Dr. Chad. Then I'd undoubtedly

begin to second-think my lie as I panicked at the thought of someone choking or falling ill. Someone across the room would loudly cry, "Is there a doctor in the house?!" Everyone at my table would point at me. "Him! He's a doctor!" I'd then have to attempt following through with my ridiculous lie. As I bumbled through the charade, everyone would know me for the fraud I'd always been.

It can be hard to put into words what you do. When someone asks me, I usually tell them some combo of writer, director, and storyteller. Yet I always feel the need to include supplemental information. Who I am and what I do can't exactly be put easily into a neat box. Nobody can. I share what I do for work, but then begin attempting to explain away who I actually am. I slowly turn into one of those troubled teens on a daytime talk show, snapping my fingers back and forth and shouting, "You don't know me! You don't know me!"

Maybe you've also had the feeling that people assumed they knew who you are based on limited information? You're at a din-

ner. All is going well. The food is wonderful. The setting is perfect. The company is superb, but then it happens. The question is asked. It's not meant to completely derail the evening, but it does because they ask:

"So, what do you do?"

There I was at this fancy dinner. We had been invited to the Jefferson Awards in Washington, D.C. Founded in 1972 by Jacqueline Kennedy Onassis, Senator Robert Taft, and Mr. Sam Beard, the awards were created to celebrate service. So, needless to say, it was an honor to be invited and have our work recognized. It was also a little out of my element and that of my young brother-in-law. Decorative nameplates were set out on each table around the room.

We found our spots by seeing our names on the place cards. I was relieved by the assigned seating. I casually wondered who they'd placed next to me. That's when I looked to discover that the person seated beside me would be none other than Justice Sonia Sotomayor of the U.S. Supreme Court.

Supreme Court justice. She is a SUPREME. COURT. JUSTICE. "So, what do you do, Supreme Court justice Sonia Sotomayor?" I'm not going to ask that. I know what she does! She does really important work . . . Supreme Court justice-ing. Come to think of it, me referring to her work as Supreme Court justice-ing is precisely the reason why I should not be allowed to sit next to her, much less speak around her.

My mind began to play out different scenarios. I again explored possibly just telling her I was a doctor, but my better judgment prevailed. Robby was playing with his napkin. I was pretending to be completely at home at the table, though wondering how I'd ever be able to tell her I just make silly YouTube videos for a living. She was, after all, someone in the midst of making history. She was making a massive difference in the world. She had even appeared on an episode of *Sesame Street*, which I'd seen with my kids—several times—and could reenact word for word.

The anticipation grew and then our tablemates all arrived. Justice Sotomayor greeted us and was, as I expected, absolutely estimable. Robby and I both successfully made it through the meal without any incidents involving food. I cautiously tried to steer any and all conversation away from interest in me or what I "do." But then—like during all other dinners or interactions with grownup people—it happened. The question. Except this time, there was a twist.

Supreme Court justice Sonia Sotomayor spoke in my direction. "So, Brad . . ."

I could feel the question coming. I could feel my shoulders tightening. *Please ask me to pass the salt,* I thought. *Please ask me to pass the salt.*

She was leaning toward me with great interest. "Tell me . . ."

Here it comes. I continued to roll around in my head. *Salt. Salt. Salt. Just ask me to pass the salt . . .*

"What do you **love** about what you do?"

Silence. *What do I love about what I do?* Did I hear that correctly? *Love?* Now this I could answer. This unlocked in me a fury of words. *I love getting to work with young people. I love getting to make things that I needed when I was a kid. I love getting to simply create. I love. I love. I love.* The words spilled out of me.

What do you **love** about what you do? Throughout the night, I heard her ask this same question of many other people. She didn't do so in a scripted or robotic way. This was an intentional, thoughtful question from an intentional, thoughtful person. I'm sure of it, because I saw her soulfully take in each answer with genuine inquisitiveness.

She even asked Robby the question. Sometimes people would speak to him as if he were more like an internet meme or some magical unicorn boy from space and not an actual person. Not her. She had no reference for the videos we made beyond what we had shared with her. She asked him, "So, Robby, what do you love about being Kid President?" I sat on edge awaiting his response. As with most young kids, there was truly no guessing what he'd say, ever. In interviews I would always be a bundle of nerves because I would never know where he might take things. At the time, it was something that distressed me. Now it's really one of my absolute favorite things about him.

Robby's response floored me. He looked at her and, after taking a moment to think, said, "I love getting to help people. I love getting to do things like this, but mostly . . ."

Oh no, I thought. *Where is he going with this?*

". . . I just like doing things with Brad."

There it was. She had invited him to put words to something I didn't know I needed to hear. Here was why he loved doing what we'd been doing. Here was why I loved what we'd been doing. We loved helping people and just being together. Plus, he said he just liked being with me. Just me, as I am.

I think I knew, deep down, that those were going to be his answers. I'd just never heard him articulate them. I wondered, also, if he'd even heard me put words to what I love about what we'd been doing together. When you get busy, you tend to just complain or assume everyone knows what you love. Somehow the most important thing about what we do and why we do it—the love—had become something we didn't speak of enough.

I remembered back to the days of lying on my office floor. The discouragements had piled up. The barrage of requests, critiques, and internet comments had caused me to lose sight of the very reasons I'd started making things in the first place. I'd forgotten what I loved about what I did, who I did it with, and why.

As the evening ended and we were saying our goodbyes, I was able to find Justice Sotomayor and thank her. I admitted feeling nervous about being seated next to her. She laughed, and I was relieved. It was encouraging also when she expressed feeling nervous about fancy dinners as well. In that moment, we were . . . just humans. Connecting and laughing as real people. Since it was doubtful we'd find ourselves together ever again, I knew I had to ask it. My time asking questions of kids had been making me a better question-asker all around. So, I tried out my new skills on her:

"So, I have a question. You asked me and many others what we *love* about what we do. Where did that come from?"

She smiled and said, "Well, when you know what somebody loves, you know who they really are."

She continued, "If I ask somebody what they do, then they'll give me a noun. People aren't really nouns, though. I want to get to know who a person really is. So, to do that, you have to get to the love."

We then talked about how she responds to the question "So, what do you do?" This was funny to me, because I assumed most people would know. However, she said a lot of people actually

HELLO, MY NAME IS SONIA, AND I HELP PEOPLE.

don't recognize her and casually ask what she does for a living. Interestingly, she said she doesn't leap to say, "Oh, I'm a Supreme Court justice!" Which, part of me feels like I would. I'd likely get T-shirts printed and vanity license plates for my car that all made certain to announce my role as someone who officially has a job for life.

When people ask her what she does, her response is not to give her title. Her response is not about her rank. Her response is who she really is, which is to say, it is what she loves. She said she tells people, "Hello, my name is Sonia, and I help people. I try to give voice to people in need. Now, how can I help you?"

It turns out that kids are like Supreme Court justices. They're looking for what you love. They're hoping there's some crossover between what they love and what you love. They're wanting to connect. Really, it's true of kids and all of us former kids. We're all just children on a playground wanting desperately to be loved and to tell one another about that love.

In classrooms I found that students would clam up when I asked for statistical information. Age? Grade? Siblings? But when I began asking questions like a child—or like Sonia Sotomayor—they would light up. I'd sometimes present them with a blank sheet of paper and ask them to fill it with all the things they love. They'd go on and on drawing animals and soccer balls and favorite books. They'd draw people they loved and write out the names of family, friends, teachers, and celebrities. By the time the activity ended, many would still be attempting to find room to place at least one more loved thing on their sheet. When the students held them up,

I looked at those once blank, lifeless sheets of paper now brightly covered in love and I'd know so much more about who'd filled them than I did before.

My conversation with Justice Sotomayor shifted how I think about what I do for a living. She dismantled how I see my own identity. Now, instead of obsessing over how my work defines me, I'm constantly making an inventory of what I love. Instead of worrying about how others will see me, I'm trying to think of ways I can make sure they feel seen. It's a process of trying to operate out of love and not out of a desire to be loved.

It is her wisdom that inspired me to try to change how I think of myself, introduce myself, and get to know others. Every day has become a quest to focus on what I **love** about what I do. On difficult days, there can be nothing better for me or for you than to stop to take stock of those things that make us who we are—those things that we love.

You and I are more than our names. We are more than our professions. We are a glorious mishmash of decisions and indecisions. We are a collection of loves and longings. Khalil Gibran said, "Work is love made visible." As someone trying to be a better grownup, I want that to be true of me. I want the things I'm doing to reflect who I really am and all that I really love.

So the next time I visited a classroom after this revelation, I began with:

"Hello! My name is Brad and I love to help people. I love telling and hearing stories from kids and former kids. What do you love about being in this class?"

CHAPTER NINE

PEP TALKS
AND
SPACE JAMS

Classrooms are unpredictable places. Aside from the fun little verbal curveballs students can throw your way, there's also the environments themselves. Sometimes you'll open the door to a themed-out wonderland or to a brightly colored edu-playground. These aren't just rooms with desks. Lots of work and planning have gone into creating safe, immersive spaces where learning can happen at every turn. Regardless of budget or school type, I'm always impressed and inspired by the love poured into these big and small details.

Walking into one school in Missouri, I quickly felt those great and familiar classroom vibes. The entire place was bright with student art lining the walls. There were designated spaces for reading and creating. It was the kind of place that immediately made me wish I were a fourth grader again.

Students were always eager to show me around, and these fourth graders were no different. A small group of kids had been chosen to be my guides for the morning. We'd already visited their library and gym, where I'd thoroughly embarrassed myself trying to do a layup. Now, standing in their classroom, a bookshelf lined with trophies caught my eye.

"Wow! Are these all awards your class has won?" I asked, pointing to the shelf.

"No, those are trophies Mrs. Reagin gave us," said one student.

She grabbed a trophy off the shelf and handed it to me.

"See," she said, smiling.

I looked at the trophy where with engraved letters it said, BEST EMMA S. AWARD. A closer glance at the shelf revealed that every single one of these trophies belonged to a student in the class. Emma explained how Mrs. Reagin had presented each of her fourth graders with a trophy at the beginning of the school year. She did this big ceremony declaring them all to be the best at being who they were. Just by being themselves, they'd done enough to be deemed worthy of a trophy displayed prominently in her classroom.

It seems silly to be jealous of a child's plastic trophy, but I was. In a culture focused heavily on grades and testing and high-achievement, I was not the kind of student who swam in awards. My grades were average. My athletic skills were troubling. Trophies are not distributed for being the awkward kid who drew cartoons about squirrels in his notebook. They did give out participation trophies and ribbons, though. My shelf at home was packed with those sorts of things.

Mrs. Reagin's trophies were different. These weren't impersonal. She presented them to each student as a way of letting them all know that, individually, they'd already earned her respect. They were already deserving of being acknowledged and celebrated. Now they could really get to work learning and growing even more together.

I'd love to travel back in time and hand a younger version of me one of those trophies. I'd return to when I was a kid growing up on the farm. Some part of me would surely want to pass on helpful hints about the future, like "Invest in this company" or "The winning lottery numbers are . . ." I'd tell myself not to let my little brother shoot me with that pellet gun. (For some reason, we thought it'd be a great idea.) I'd try to prevent myself from heartache or failure. Yet maybe one of the most important things I could tell that younger me is, "You're really good at being you. This world needs *you*. Be *you*. Grow from there."

Time travel, thankfully, does not exist. I'm far too poor at making decisions to be allowed that kind of responsibility. Maybe all of humanity is. It sure would be nice, though, to be able to slip ourselves some useful notes on living, like kids covertly swapping cheat sheets for a math test. But that's not how growth works.

Up until this Listening Tour, I'd been exhausting myself with work. My biggest fear was being insignificant, and so to combat that, I was determined to do something of significance. Somehow, fundamentally, I felt I was just not enough. My thinking was that maybe—just maybe—if I did enough important things, then I'd prove my worth. Then I would be enough. Then I'd be a success.

I was wrong. I was wrong about my worth and I was wrong about success. I learned this by becoming "successful" and finding I still didn't feel like I was enough.

It all started because I wrote a pep talk. I write pep talks because I need pep talks. Back in school, my notebooks had encouraging words scattered throughout them. I'd scrawl encouraging messages on corner pages as bits of inspiration to help me deal with being in middle school. This continued in college with notecards taped onto my giant desktop computer, scraps of paper with motivating words on them left in my car, or underlined sentences in favorite books with the hope that I'd discover them again at later dates. Once, at a time in my life when I thought my most exciting days were behind me, I wrote and filmed a pep talk.

Back when I started creating videos with my little brother-in-law, I didn't see our *Kid President* project going beyond the circle of friends in our community. Yet with each week, our audience for these videos grew. This reached what I thought would be its most impressive crescendo in November 2012, just as the U.S. presidential election was wrapping up. By that time, we had created about eighteen videos, gotten a lot of national and international press, met some really cool people, and—most of all—had a lot of fun. In my mind, this was the end. Now with the election over, we'd close the book on this chapter, and my regularly scheduled life would resume.

Rainn Wilson, known to many for his role as Dwight on the popular television series *The Office*, had become one of our biggest cheerleaders. The media company he'd helped create, SoulPancake, had teamed up with me to help us reach even more people. I loved the idea of continuing to work with them to put videos filled with heart and hope out into the world, but I couldn't see how it was going to happen. The election was over, and I figured that meant nobody would be interested in a tiny president. Even so, my new friends at SoulPancake asked me to continue making videos. "At least just until January," they suggested.

As the new year arrived, I was writing and preparing to film what I thought would be the final batch of *Kid President* videos. Since these were the last ones we'd be making, I wanted to be a little more ambitious. It was a long shot, but my thinking was that maybe if I made something strong enough, then Rainn and the SoulPancake team would let me keep working with them.

On top of that, I wanted to make something that really mattered. Right in the middle of all this, my wife and I were welcoming our first child into the world. Suddenly, I didn't just want to do good work or get a good job. I began to hope that one day this baby would grow up to see the stuff his old man was making. Even at just a few weeks old, this little baby had me wanting to make him proud. Parenthood makes your brain weird, okay?

Normally, Kid President remained behind a little desk. For this, I thought it'd be fun to break free from the confines of the cardboard Oval Office and see this character experiencing the world. I'd spend a little more time with each shot. I'd soak in the fun. I'd focus on the gratitude I felt in getting to create something I believed in with someone I loved. I thought that maybe, many years from now, my son would see this and find visible proof of what his dad cared about. He'd watch his father's and uncle's love for each other and see the hope we held for the future. In a way, the video was made for an audience of one.

Much like the pep talks I'd been writing for myself all those years, I wrote a pep talk for Kid President to deliver. It was going to be so different from the things we'd made before that I began to second-guess the whole idea.

I had written an outline with the key elements for it on a note-card and, in a moment of self-doubt, thrown it in the garbage. But with a deadline looming and no better ideas popping up, I fished the pep talk out of the trash. This would have to be how Robby and I would close out our *Kid President* project together.

It was a cold Tennessee January when we filmed. The local high school football field was brown and empty, leaving us with plenty of space to do our thing. Robby had never set foot on a football field before and was thrilled to run where—in his words—"real football guys" had been tackled. We were both delighted to be out and about together. It felt new and exciting. I was sad that it had to end.

While uploading all the footage, I realized I had nearly two and half hours of stuff to comb through. This would need to be edited down to two minutes. Undaunted, I crafted and shaped it into what I hoped would be a blast of optimism. I was energized by the thrill of preparing a big and hopeful pep talk for an unsuspecting internet. Then the power went out. Also, a large tree fell on my house. While I was working, I heard a loud boom mixed with a crunching sound. I stepped outside to see a giant tree on my roof. Did I mention we had a newborn in our home who woke up when things like this happened? I didn't feel like creating a pep talk anymore; I needed one.

That video, "A Pep Talk from Kid President to You," was posted online on a Thursday evening. By Sunday, it had a million views. Then three million. Then it kept going. It's still going. At this writing, it has been viewed more than forty-four million times. We quickly found ourselves on the *Today* show, CNN, *Good Morning America*, MSNBC, and on and on and on. Somehow my cell phone number got out. My inbox was filled with requests. People reached out to say they'd been moved by the video. One guy even wrote in to say, "Hey, I watched your pep talk and I quit my job." Oh no.

How had this happened? It was just a video. While I did want it to be special, I didn't necessarily want it to be this special. I definitely didn't intend on pushing people to quit their jobs. But this was more than just a video. This was a runaway train.

When something goes viral, it circulates so rapidly and so extensively there's no way of even beginning to process the *why* or *how*. Sometimes things get passed around because viewers are

shocked and they want others to be shocked. Sometimes things get passed around because viewers are outraged and they want others to be outraged. Sometimes things get passed around because that one kid in daycare didn't cover his mouth when he coughed. (This is an entirely different kind of viral, but it does apply because the internet can be a gross place sometimes.)

We share things because we want to relay feelings. We want not to be alone. Now, many years removed from the video's release, people still tell me, sometimes with tears in their eyes, how this video made them feel. It is something I'll spend a lifetime trying to comprehend. I'm grateful it meant something to others, as it definitely meant something to me. The viral nature of this pep talk helped me realize I wasn't alone. I wasn't the only one in the world who needed some encouragement. It was also a lovely reminder that many things are contagious—anger, fear, yawns. But hope, love, and joy are the best kind of contagious. Good can, and does, spread.

One of the lines I wrote for that pep talk video was this:

"Don't quit! What if Michael Jordan had quit when he didn't make the team in high school? He would've never made Space Jam. *And I love* Space Jam.

"What will be your Space Jam? *What will you create that will make the world more awesome?"*

What will be your *Space Jam*? What will be that thing you create that you will be remembered for forever? I thought the line was funny and surprising. It meant a lot to me, as a fan of the 1996 Bugs Bunny–Michael Jordan film. Sure, Michael Jordan had done historic things in the NBA, but for me, as a non–sports fan, his saving the planet from aliens with the cast of Looney Tunes was what really captured my heart. It also felt like a powerful challenge to throw out to my fellow humans, perhaps the greatest challenge of all: What will be your *Space Jam*? What will you create that will prove your significance on this planet?

I had no idea just how much that line would come to haunt me. It forced me to ask myself a series of very tough questions. It has led to many sleepless nights. It's part of the reason I ended up just lying on my office floor with no clue what to do next. While I was grateful for the many ways that pep talk video resonated with so many people at the level it did, it left me wondering:

That time we met the president

Did I make my *Space Jam*? Is that pep talk video the biggest thing I'll ever do? Am I done? Do I just . . . die now?

"What will be your *Space Jam*?" no longer sounded to me like a rallying cry for creating work that matters but instead became an albatross. Those once encouraging words were now a giant burden on my back that nothing could remove. I had gone from needing a pep talk to writing a pep talk to suddenly, again, feeling like this pep talk would haunt me for the rest of my life.

There are many things I've made since that video. In fact, we released a video nearly every single week after that. Many of them did really well, but very few of them reached the heights of the pep talk. That video was parodied on television shows. It was watched by President Barack Obama—who even invited us to the real Oval Office. It led to a series of miraculous events that I'm still scratching my head about. Yet even as incredible opportunities came across my path, I couldn't shake the feeling that I'd already made my *Space Jam*. Nothing else good would happen to me.

Great things did continue to come across my path, though. The United Nations invited me to create a short film for a project whose mission was to help people understand its Global Goals Initiative. I was elated. The video challenged me as a writer and director, plus it was something I very much believed in. The U.N.

invited me to come to New York, where the film would be screened and I would deliver a brief introduction to it. We flew the whole family out for this. I went backstage at the event, and instead of a warm greeting, they looked at me with total confusion. This is when I let them know that I was the important person who'd been invited to give an important speech before showing the important film I had made for them. You know, because I'm important. These were not the words I used, but it's how I felt. A stagehand with a clipboard scuttled away and returned with a strange look. Then she said it:

THE U.N. NEEDED MY HELP.

"We forgot."

They forgot I was going to do the speech. The wheels of the program were already so far in motion and they couldn't stop them. The video played without my introduction and I walked from backstage to find my family. Then we went back to the hotel. The next day we flew home. The end!

That's not what I shared on social media, though. Online I shared a picture of me standing in front of the United Nations building with the caption: "I got invited to the U.N.!" I left out the part where they forgot about me and the part where I cried. This is all so embarrassing to share, even now. It's not a bad problem to have, being forgotten by the U.N. Why did I even care? I'd been perfectly fine in my life before I knew they wanted me to speak. Now that this had been presented to me as an option and taken away, I was suddenly hurt by it. Silly, I know. There are far bigger problems one can have.

That question continued popping up and replaying on a loop in my head, though: What will be your *Space Jam*? All this had tapped into something very primal inside me—wanting to know I mattered. I worked and worked to develop new projects. As I pitched them, people would politely listen and then in the end reveal they only really wanted this fictional character of Kid President. Somewhere deep down, I knew that my significance had nothing to do with the things I made or did. It's hard to remember that, though, when the world seems to be shouting about just one thing you've done.

Home from the United Nations, I continued to work. We took on a project to help schools in our community. It was a project I loved because it allowed me to do something inspiring apart from the internet. This was something that would provide resources for a real school in real life. An area newspaper did a short article about the project, which was great. The only problem was that they misspelled my name. Several times. Many different ways.

I laughed about the misspelling with my wife. It was all part of how these things go. But I found myself continually bringing it up. This typo began to infect my brain. In my tired, twisted thinking, these tiny misplaced letters weren't mistakes; they were giant announcements from the world that I was insignificant. I did not matter, my name did not matter, and nothing I'd ever do could or would ever matter. So silly, I know.

After I brought up the misspelled name for probably the hundredth time, Kristi brought me back to reality: "This isn't why you do this."

It hit me. With a fistful of love, those words hit me. Getting my name spelled correctly wasn't the point. That isn't why I took on that project. I didn't start any of this so that I could get in our local newspaper or give a speech to the United Nations or have a video make people want to quit their jobs. I never set out to make things for any purpose other than I just love to do it. For the love of loving and the joy of expressing joy. Just as Justice Sotomayor had reminded me, it was all about love.

Making things as an act of love is what I do when I'm at my best. I made that pep talk out of love, not for lights and attention. As a kid, I used to color not because I wanted applause or approval, but just because I wanted to mix all the colors together to see what would happen. Sometimes, as icing on the cake, my mom would put the art up on our refrigerator. That didn't make me more significant, though. In my mother's eyes I already mattered. This was just a bonus.

So those words came back to me: "What will be your *Space Jam*? What will you create to make the world more awesome?"

It was all a long road to figuring out that my *Space Jam* is not one thing I make. My *Space Jam* is my life. Same for you. Your *Space Jam* isn't one thing you do. It's a steady work in progress. Your *Space Jam* is your entire life and you get only one life, so

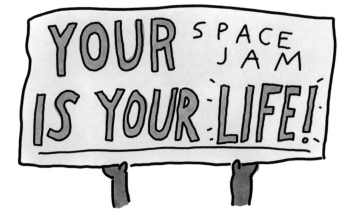

make it a good one. I'd travel back in time and let my former self know all this. I'd pass a little note that says, "YOUR *SPACE JAM* IS YOUR LIFE!" He wouldn't get it, though. It doesn't make sense unless you've lived through it. Life's that way, I guess.

Becoming a better grownup is not about achieving more. Part of being a better grownup is letting people know they are enough—including yourself. It's realizing that every single day is another layer of fresh color on the masterpiece of a life you're painting. It's handing out trophies to let people know they've wowed you by simply being the best at who they are. Maybe it's even creating a trophy for yourself, holding it, and owning it.

One day on the Listening Tour, I showed a group of fourth graders in Oregon the notecard that I'd written the pep talk script on, thrown away, and then pulled out of the trash can. It was one of those "Follow your heart! Trust your gut!" moments. I explained how I'd jotted down the notes for what would become the pep talk video. The scrap had creases and wrinkles from where I'd tossed it in the trash and carried it around in the years since. I explained to them how, at one point, I didn't feel like the video would work. Then, feeling the responsibility to be totally honest with them, I shared how I was feeling at that exact moment. "So I made this thing, and lots of people loved it. What if I never make anything great ever again?"

There was a pause. I'd learned to accept these quiet moments in conversations like this. I was less accepting of pauses in my career or other aspects of my life. In conversations with students, pauses can mean they don't quite have an answer yet. Usually it means they're really, deeply thinking. Wonderful things nearly always come after these extended pauses. I'm trying to remember this in every area of my life.

The Listening Tour had taught me that kids appreciated when I was honest and opened up. They enjoyed wrestling with big ideas and, more often than not, had remarkable insight. Today was no different. A young boy named Darius spoke up and said, "Well, babies start crawling and have no idea that they're gonna get to walk soon. They don't even know what walking is." He smiled and some of his fellow classmates laughed, since his analogy seemed to come out of nowhere. A young girl named Alex chimed in, "I'm glad I didn't stop after crawling, because I wouldn't have ever run or ridden a bike."

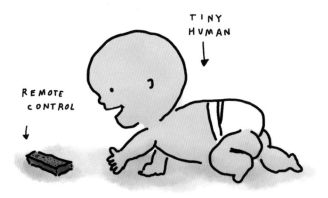

One very normal afternoon shortly after that, I was at home playing with both my kids. They were crawling all over me and playing a game they called "birthday." In this game, whether it is your birthday or not, you are celebrated to the fullest extent of their imaginations. First, they would declare it your birthday. Then, in celebration, they would dump things on you. Celebrating for seemingly no reason and creating a giant mess are favorite pastimes for most toddlers. So, to "celebrate" my "birthday," I had the honor of having pillows and toys dropped on my head. They soon graduated from dropping pillows and toys to dropping larger items like books and even emptying out my bag in search of more ammunition for celebration. This is when I stepped out of my role of "birthday boy" and back into dad mode.

Attempting to get all my work stuff back where it belonged, I noticed something. In the pile of stuff from my bag being thrown on top of me, there was a notecard. It was the little notecard with the pep talk written on it. They didn't know what it was. Honestly, they didn't care. Neither of these little humans had any clue what that pep talk video was or what was written on that card. I'd made that video to try to somehow impress them. They didn't know how many views my latest video had. Honestly, they wouldn't care or be the slightest bit impressed if they did know. That's not why they were crawling all over me. They just know and love me as me. They love me for who I am in that moment. That's it.

I cannot pass this information or a trophy on to my former self via time travel, but I can slip this note to you: Sometimes we spend so much time doing things for applause or approval that we miss out on the love that's right in front of us already. That pep talk video has been seen by millions of people. My best work, though, will never be seen by that many. Sure, I might create something else that connects with a large audience. My best work, though? It will always happen in the interactions that are one-on-one, face-to-face with the people right beside me.

Maybe you're discouraged. Keep making anyway. Your best work might not be fully recognized. Keep making anyway. You might be misunderstood. You might feel forgotten or ignored or have your name misspelled in the newspaper. Keep making anyway. Yes, you might create something as great as *Space Jam*, but guess what? Your *Space Jam* isn't something you create. Your *Space Jam* is something you live. This masterpiece is a work in progress. Maybe you're just at the part where you're crawling. Maybe you've only just reached the part where you're walking. Wherever you are, it all adds up to something magnificent.

It's you. You're the work of art. You might make or do brilliant, beautiful things in your lifetime, but nothing is more remarkable than the simple fact that you are here and you are you.

So go live a masterpiece of life so full of hope and love and joy that it lights up the world.

Go live your *Space Jam*.

CHAPTER
TEN

HOW TO
GROW

Over the course of all the visits with classrooms, I heard a lot of words. Through it all, there was one that stood out. It's a word I heard many times from more than one educator and one I've tried to make part of my daily vocabulary. The first time was when the teacher thoughtfully interrupted a student who was talking. The student had just told me that he couldn't play any instruments.

"*Yet*," the teacher interrupted. "You can't play any instruments . . . *yet*."

It was a small moment between teacher and student, but a big lesson I needed to hear. Three letters making up one very small little word. *Yet* can change how we think about ourselves and all that is possible. Who we are today does not have to be who we are tomorrow. We are not the grownups we can be . . . yet.

I learned that many schools were incorporating the idea of a growth mindset. The term comes from professor and researcher Carol Dweck, whose studies in the psychology of motivation and success revealed the massive significance found in how we frame our abilities. A person can go through life with a fixed mindset, thinking they are forever only capable of what they can do now. Many people do this, but they're stuck. With a growth mindset, there's no end to what someone might be able to do. It's the idea that we can always be learning and advancing, in every area of our lives. A tough patch is not an automatic failure; it's a challenge. We just have to be willing to grow.

While some people might dismiss it as a mere buzzword, a *growth mindset* goes beyond being a trend. Many educators have altered their approach to all their work because of it. Schools have always strived to be places where people grow, but Dweck's work has prompted many to create cultures and environments where students are passionate about stretching and growing, forever. One principal described it as an attempt to create "lifelong learners beyond the classroom." The idea definitely began to have an effect on me.

I was reminded of how terrifying school could be at times. Trying something new, and knowing there are people watching—classmates you want to impress—well, that can be mortifying. You want to look smart! I wondered if maybe all these educators remembered just how uncomfortable it is to take that risk. While so many other grownups might have forgotten what school could be like, these teachers were creating safe spaces for students to say, "I don't know." And as these students said this, the teachers were all gently adding, ". . . yet. You don't know this yet."

One teacher told me his fear of failure is actually what led him to a career working with students. Describing himself from early elementary school until junior high, he said, "I was so afraid of messing things up. I wanted everything to be perfect." Mr. Paul, as the students call him now, worked to have perfect penmanship, perfect report cards, and even perfect attendance. However, in junior high, a science teacher changed the way he thought about school forever.

"This teacher divided us into groups. He passed around all these different experiments we had to do together. Then he stood at the front of the class and watched with glee as every single one of them failed."

The teacher had purposely given them all instructions for experiments that would not succeed.

"I remember being on the verge of tears. I'd followed his steps word for word. I did everything exactly as it should've been done, and it was a disaster—a glorious disaster."

Now, "glorious disasters" are a key part of what he does. Like his mad scientist teacher before him, Mr. Paul begins each school year by setting his students up for experiments that will fail. While that might sound sadistic, he knows what a gift failure was for him when he was a student. Failing, done correctly, is learning. The students begin questioning instructions they're given, they gain an understanding of how experiments work, and they gain a bold new spirit of curiosity about what might happen next.

I've spent a lot of time in my life worried about what might happen next, especially recently. Following the viral success of the pep talk, I'd become petrified of making any further moves for fear that one of them might be the wrong one. A failed experiment in a

°ACHIEVE°

Even this sloth is more productive than you.

classroom is one thing, but the stakes were higher here in grownup land. A fruitless business venture or an unsuccessful creative endeavor could have far-reaching consequences, not just for me but also for my family.

The weight of all of this, mixed with exhaustion and a deep depression I'd never known before, had pulled me down to a place that I didn't think I'd ever find my way out of. It was a dark, scary place where, for lack of any other decision-making abilities, I ate way too many Oreos.

Now, on the other side of that, I can see all that I've learned and all the ways that I've grown. It's just . . . growing isn't always fun. It's actually really painful most of the time.

Mr. Paul's classroom, like many others I visited, was lined with posters encouraging students to be inspired by the examples of famous failures. Images of brilliant minds like Albert Einstein with words about how he wasn't a great student, or a poster of *Harry Potter* author J. K. Rowling sharing that her manuscript was rejected twelve times. They'd both done okay for themselves. I'd heard those stories before, but I wondered if Albert Einstein or J. K. Rowling ever ate way too many Oreos. I was certain my unique ability to fail spectacularly and make poor decisions far outweighed their talents as famous failures.

Mari Andrew is an illustrator and a friend who shared something I think about all the time. She opened up about a family friend who had died the week before. She said so many people talked about him in big, beautiful ways. She wrote this: "People described him as the 'most compassionate human of all time.' I'm blown away by that legacy. This morning I'm thinking about how I want to be remembered and working backwards."

I was pretty far into my listening project and had focused solely on kids. It'd been life-giving to hear their perspectives, and they'd brought me back to seeing the world with childlike eyes. Over and over I'd heard thoughts from them about how I could be a better grownup and, until now, I hadn't thought to interview any people who'd actually grown up.

So I wondered if I could do a little experiment. I'd begin to interview a few older people, adding them into the Listening Tour. Specifically, of course, people who didn't make aging look miserable. I'd seek out a few men and women who'd grown and aged gracefully, make notes on what I wanted to implement from their lives, and, if my experiment wasn't a disaster, from there I could just . . . work backward.

As I started this new phase, I also had to come face-to-face with something: I didn't know or spend much time with many people who were much older than myself. This was due to a slight fear, maybe. You don't want to bother people who are older. They're busy doing older-people things. I also didn't know what to talk about. The biggest reason, though, had to be that I didn't want to do or say anything wrong. I guess, even though I'm an adult now, some part of me still has a fear of getting in trouble.

Walker had never made me feel this way. I decided he'd be the perfect person to start with for a number of reasons. Number one, I know him and he knows me. My wife and I were friends with him and had worked at camp with some of his grandkids. Now we lived in the same town, and he always made a point to check in and see what I was working on or how things were going with me. It always surprised me that he even knew my name.

My friend Walker Whittle is a veteran of World War II, well into his nineties, a retired business professor, and an incredibly active member of our small community. I make silly videos on the internet. Sometimes unlikely friendships are the best kind.

A few weeks before I connected with him to be interviewed, he was trying to convince me to buy a giant ham. The ham was for a fundraiser he was organizing. Mr. Whittle was heavily involved in our local Civitans, a volunteer group dedicated to meeting and serving needs in communities around the world. This was just one of the many ways he stayed busy. He was committed to his deeply held faith and also very interested in cooking, traveling, and reading. Often our discussions were about whatever book he was reading at that time. He claimed to devour three books each week, and I believed him. His interests ranged from old baseball players to theology to history to whatever else he could get his hands on.

He'd seen many things in his ninety-five years. He had count-less fascinating stories about his time in the service. One thing that always surprised me was the superb de-tail with which he could recall elements from his time in World War II to his time teaching, including particular students, names, and situations. He could even still tell vivid sto-ries about his days as a child. When I arranged to meet up with him, I let him know this project was about my attempting to gain wisdom from listening to kids and, now, former kids. He came prepared with a list.

So these are the "chapters of life." He smiled as he shared them, but there was also great caution in

MR. WHITTLE
(veteran, retired educator,
amazing grownup)

his voice. It was as if he'd seen many people go through this life adventure, himself among them. These few words he'd typed out were the result of lots of experience.

THE CHAPTERS OF LIFE
(according to Mr. Whittle, age 95½)

Infancy: A period of innocence

Youth: A period of discovery

13–19: A period of uncertainty, yet decision

20–30: A period of direction and wonder

30–40: A period of production and expectation

40–70: A period of regret or rejoicing

70 and beyond: A period of satisfaction and seeking

At first, I was thrilled. Here I was wanting my life to be my *Space Jam*, and he was outlining all the chapters for me. These chapters, however, didn't exactly sound thrilling. Easier, calmer chapters would've been nice. You know, chapters where it's me not having to do anything, people just bringing me really good food, and everything always working out for the best. The end!

Curious, I dug a bit more. "So, all the chapters are already determined? I don't get to choose what happens? Am I stuck with these?" I asked.

"Each chapter has choices," he said with a grin.

"But what about the things that happen that are completely out of my control?" I asked, as if I was actually going to stump a ninety-five-year-old man.

"There's parts of the story you don't get to choose," he again said with that smile. "But you do get to decide how you'll respond. Those decisions shape every chapter after that."

Decisions. Sometimes even just deciding what my wife and I will eat for dinner can send me in a panic. To my ears, *decision* is a scary word like *ax murderer* or *clown* or *incoming call*. My decision aversion has upset my wife on plenty of occasions. In fact, I rarely call anyone on my phone—even her. It's as if I'm constantly afraid my decision to call will create some catastrophic chain of events or, worse, *bother someone*.

I don't want to be a bother. I don't want to be bothered. I don't want to make a decision that might bother me, someone else, or the universe at large. Decisions have consequences and I don't want consequences.

But again and again, decisions would come up in every conversation I had with any older friends I spoke with. Starting with Walker, they'd all talk about good decisions and bad decisions. These decisions have really stuck with them, too. Some decisions, as Walker suggested, result in great rejoicing; and some, in deep, painful regret.

"But what if I make the wrong choice? Mr. Walker, what if I fail?" I asked him.

"Don't worry," he told me. "You will fail."

Not exactly the encouraging words I'd been hoping to hear from my older, wiser friend. Didn't he know I was the pep talk guy? I write pep talks. I need pep talks. This was not a pep talk. However, he knew I needed it, and he knew I could handle it. Failure is inevitable. Failure, done correctly, is learning. It's growing. Deal with it, kid.

He told me his pro-failing stance is one of the things that's helped him grow and one of the things he continually tries to instill in his children, grandchildren, and great-grandchildren.

"Keep trying and learning. Failure is part of the process. It means you're living."

So, failing means I'm living. To a degree, that's freeing to hear. It means I'm pretty alive at the moment. It's okay to mess up. It's part of the process. But these decisions have weight. There are consequences, right? Walker's chapters-of-life breakdown even outlines it.

"So, thirty years of regret or rejoicing, huh?" I asked.

"Well, it's obviously different for each person, but I've found it to be true," he said, pausing to add an important disclaimer. "Good news, though: You can also start over at any time!"

"There are do-overs?!" I excitedly asked.

"Yes. There are do-overs."

Discussing fears and dreams with elementary school students could sometimes remind me how much weight our choices have even at a young age. Sometimes students brought up issues and troubles I'd forgotten were part of being a child. "I used to sit alone at lunch," shared one boy named Jarrett. He had a strength and a sadness in his eyes as he added, "but now I have some friends here and I've been nicer. So that's good." It sounds like he's getting a do-over, but it was so tough to hear this kid open up about his trouble making and keeping friends. "I've been nicer," he said. That's the part that killed me. He's trying, really trying. He spoke like he was making progress, but I could hear in his voice and see by his classmates' reactions that he likely had lots of difficult days ahead of him. He still had some junk to figure out. It brought back every remembrance I ever had of feeling not up to the task of being a good-enough person even to sit by someone or deserve a friend. I'd felt like Jarrett before.

Our memories are sometimes short, and we can easily forget how difficult growing can be. We have these colorful recollections of the fun and freedom of it all but sometimes draw a blank when it comes to the frustrations found in that time of figuring life out. Unprompted in every listening session would be words from some fragile student that reminded me of the confusion and terror of being young: "I'm afraid everyone will laugh at me." "My parents don't let me do anything." "I wish I were better at tests." "Nobody understands me." They shared bewilderment and doubt, much in the same way any human of any age would, simply at how to get around in this world as a person.

In video games when you "level up," you become something new. You're the same character, be it Mario or Princess Toadstool or whoever, except you've leveled up. This means you're bigger now. You have more powers. Sometimes leveling up also means

you get cool stuff. You're the same person, but now . . . *you can do more.* This idea is not only exciting; it's also thrilling to watch. The moment you level up in a video game is full of triumphant music and graphics. Time stops. Your character usually freezes in the air, surrounded by flashes of light. All is as it should be . . . in the game, at least.

In real life, true growth isn't glamorous. It's gritty. It doesn't happen in an instant. True *leveling up* requires patience and effort. It's much more than just pushing the right combination of buttons.

So often the metaphor of a caterpillar becoming a butterfly is used when talking about our growth and development. For me, though, this story has perpetuated the idea that we would enter adulthood and be done. I've had this false expectation that I'd become a grownup all at once. I'd arrive fully formed and ready to flutter through the sky in all my butterfly glory.

Lately, though, I've been thinking a lot about lobsters. I'd seen people pass around an image online claiming that lobsters could live forever. The information was presented as if it were common knowledge, but it was totally new to me. As someone with a great interest in living forever, I began to inquire further.

What I found out is this: Lobsters are not immortal. They do, however, age in a very different way from how we and most any other animal age. Unlike people, lobsters don't really slow down as they get older. They keep growing and growing until they die. (Either from natural causes or a predator or a freak boat accident in which the lobster steals a boat and realizes it cannot drive.)

So how do lobsters do this? Well, they grow by molting, but specifically from something called ecdysis. *Ecdysis*—which is Greek for "putting off"—is the art of escaping their old shell. In order to grow, the lobster's shell must be put away so it can grow a new one. Sounds simple enough, right?

Every lobster could stay as it is, but that would mean death. Imagine the pressure the lobster must feel, being bigger on the inside than their outer shell can contain. The lobster begins to break their shell and then must complete the harrowing process of crawling out of it. The process leaves the lobster exhausted and exposed. This is an extremely dangerous time for our lobster friend. It is at extreme risk of infection or being eaten. For protection, the lobster hides in a dark place as it rests and heals, waiting for its new shell to grow.

Then, one day, everything is different. Our brave lobster has a shiny new shell. It emerges back into the busy life of the ocean, bigger and stronger than before—at least until it grows out of the newer shell and must go through this entire process all over again. And again. And again. And again.

Lobsters are in a constant state of growth. On average, a lobster goes through the molting process forty-four times before its first birthday. Then it gets in a rhythm of doing this once every few years. For lobsters, life is the perpetual process of becoming new. They spend most of their time either preparing for shedding their old shell or recovering from it. Preparing for growth or healing from growth— that's their life. Maybe, if we're doing it right, that's our life, too.

As if that weren't shocking enough to discover, the lobsters aren't precious about their old shells, either. Do you know what they do with them? *They eat them.* They use the old shell for nourishment as they heal and the new shell hardens. Maybe instead of being nostalgic about all our past pains and successes, or in lieu of carrying them around with us, we could let them all become fuel for our journey. We're best served by carrying only more wisdom and more strength into each future moment of our lives. Preparing for growth and healing for growth. That's the secret. Of course, we can only do this if we choose to have the daring determination of a lobster.

Maybe this is why some people grow older with such a fixed mindset. They're hard. They're stuck, hampered, and cramped in the hard shell they refuse to shake off. I get it, though. It's understandable. Growing into the fullness of who we are meant to be requires risk. It's gross. It is not elegant. It's hard. It takes everything we've got. We want to maintain our dignity and stick with what we know. But a refusal to grow is an offense to the natural way of things.

If you still have a pulse, you have a chance to grow. We're all amateurs, rookies, apprentices, and beginners in some area of life. I'm learning how to keep growing and embrace it with a childlike enthusiasm, even if it makes me uncomfortable—especially if it makes me uncomfortable. This means feeling like you're putting on new shoes that are a little too big, but that's a good place to be. You'll grow into them. Stumble around awkwardly in those floppy shoes. Learn how to move through life in those floppy shoes. Dance clumsily until they fit just right and it comes time to burst out of them and get new ones. Even if you don't feel like you belong in them. Life is an ongoing experiment in realizing just how qualified you are for the position of you—how perfectly cast you are in the role of yourself. You're just growing into it.

In one classroom I visited, a boy named Jameson, age nine, told me this:

"To be a grownup means to have a good life."

I agree. A few months after my last conversation with him, Mr. Walker Whittle died. His death came as a shock to most all who knew him, even though he was ninety-six. The man was full of life until the very end.

Walker liked to make lists. He made grocery lists, book lists, and, most important, life lists. I'd collected many of his little sayings and quips of advice over the years but had forgotten about this list. When he passed away, I found myself returning to his words of wisdom and especially treasured one he called "Walker Whittle's Life List (regarding wisdom and encouragement)." The list reflects his desire to live a life of service and of kindness. It speaks to his profound and personal faith, and it was a work in progress until he passed.

Walking into his memorial service, I carried with me his wisdom written on a few small sheets of paper. It was a true celebration of a life well lived with a standing-room-only crowd. As I made it through the line to see his family, I found his great-grandchildren. He was proud of them and had every reason to be. I hugged them and then handed each a little sheet of paper containing their great-grandfather's "Life List." Like the answers to some great test, it gave us something wonderful from which we could all work backward. An experiment that wouldn't fail but that would lead to glorious growth. Again and again and again and again.

WALKER WHITTLE'S LIFE LIST
(REGARDING WISDOM and ENCOURAGEMENT)

1. DO NOT BE AFRAID.

2. TRUST.

3. PRAY FREQUENTLY. (You don't have to be on your knees to pray.)

4. HAVE SOME VALUES that are UNCHANGEABLE.

5. RECOGNIZE your LIMITATIONS without STRESSING YOURSELF OUT.

6. TREAT YOUR FELLOW MAN LIKE YOU WOULD LIKE to BE TREATED.

7. COMMEND and COMPLIMENT the SUCCESS of OTHERS.

8. DO FOR OTHERS WITHOUT EXPECTING ANYTHING in RETURN.

9. BE KIND and COURTEOUS.

10. LET the LIGHT be YOUR LIFE be YOUR DAILY LIVING.

* NONE of THESE ARE WORTHWHILE unless GOD is NUMBER 1.

part three

THE GREAT
REMEMBERING

And so life moved along
as life is known to do.
So much had been forgotten,
so much they all once knew.

But we never are too distant.
We're never just too far
to come back and remember
who we really are.

Her dad was on the highway
as he tried to find a way
through knots of snarled-up traffic
so he could see her that day.

He rushed as he was able,
pushing every single limit,
because a grandson was arriving
at precisely any minute!

Though time had divided them,
today there would be joy.
The daughter was now giving birth
to a baby boy.

As she looked upon her baby,
and did so lovingly,
she suddenly saw something
she never dreamed she'd see.

How in the world?
Who could think it?
A happily floating baby
with a floating baby blanket?

The daughter, a new mother,
shook at what she saw.
And in that moment,
yes, that moment,
she remembered it all.

She

      remembered

          the

              floating,

the soaring,

the flying.

The lightness,

the laughing,

the stopping,

the crying.

She remembered how she glided
over fields and over water
but most of all—

        yes, most of all—

        she thought about her father.

It was in that instant.
It was then she finally knew.
Him. It was him—
he was why she flew.

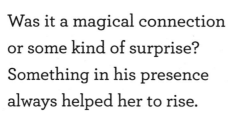

Was it a magical connection
or some kind of surprise?
Something in his presence
always helped her to rise.

She remembered how he stood by
with eyes full of care.
Never did she fly
unless he was there.

Thinking back to flying
and the magic she once knew,
she was like her father
with her child floating, too.

Just then the room's door opened,
and, I tell you, as it did,

the daughter saw her father,

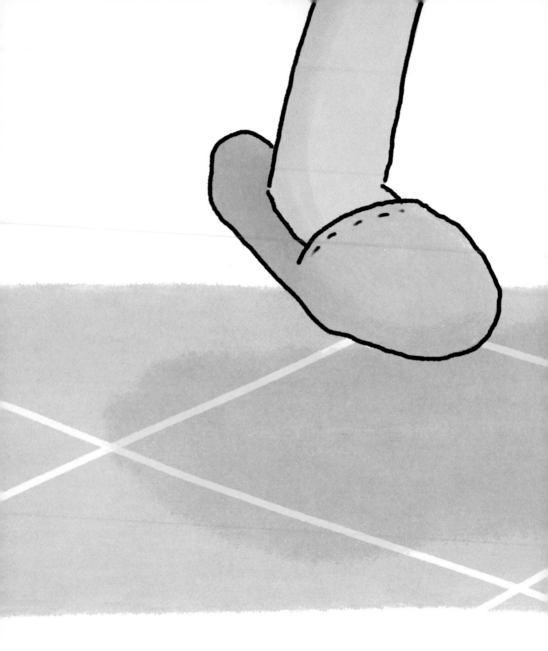

and he looked

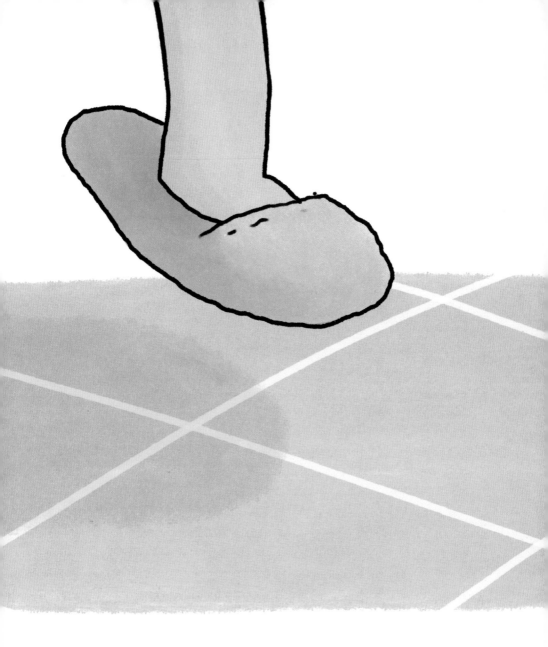

to see

her lift.

May we all remember
the magic we have known,
and never forget we need each other.
No person flies alone.

Should your spark start to fade
because of stress or time or fear,
you'll need reminding of your flying
and the reasons we are here.

To fly and help each other fly—
it's wild and it is true.
To fly and help each other fly
is what we're here to do.

CHAPTER ELEVEN

GROWNUPS
NEEDED

ANSWERING
the CALL

"You get older and older and older and older and then you die." These were the words of Morgan, age eight. It seemed an especially dark perspective on life coming from a third grader. I found myself making the kind of face you make when you've just heard nails on a chalkboard. She had somehow captured all the agony and astonishment of the human condition in just a handful of words. All I'd done was ask, "What does it mean to grow up?" We get older and we get older and then *pfffft* the end. The entire classroom giggled. I winced.

It is true: Growing up is a fatal condition. Surely, though, there's more to being alive than just getting older and older and then dying. This idea that aging is terrible, unavoidable, and leads only to death has been passed down from generation to generation. Much in the same way families pass down heirloom necklaces or prized handkerchiefs or heart disease, we pass down ideas of what it means to age. Advertisements promote products that promise they will "fight aging." Filters for photos smooth out our skin, taking years off our complexions. We compliment older people by telling them they "look so young." It makes sense that we want to stay stuck in adolescence. The alternative, marching unphotogenically to the grave, is not appealing.

Aside from Morgan's morbid response, there were other insights. According to Sofia, "To be a grownup means to be eighteen

and older," the legal definition of being an adult in the United States. But the age students gave me for what it means to be a grownup varied from student to student and school to school. For some it was twenty and others eighty-five. They didn't seem to have a clear handle on the precise number. According to one study done by the Marist Institute for Public Opinion, the students' ideas about adulthood mirror another widespread source of confusion.* If you ask a baby boomer what old is, they'll respond seventy-seven. If you ask someone from Generation X, they'll respond seventy-one. If you ask a millennial, they'll tell you sixty-two.

The same study found that when people were asked what age they hoped to live to, the average number was around ninety. We may all differ on what old is and have complicated ideas about what it looks like, but we are united by at least one thing: We'd all like to live long, happy lives. So, what is it that we're all aging toward? Do we just live and start getting slower and more feeble until we can't move? Do you just exist and keep existing until, as my third-grade friend and philosopher-queen Morgan, age eight, says, "you die?"

In spite of all this mystery and uncertainty, I'd found there were still lots of kids who couldn't wait for their turn to grow older. Inspired by the *Kid President* concept, several students regularly

*Marist Institute for Public Opinion, *Generation to Generation: Gauging the Golden Years* (2011). Retrieved from www.homeinstead.com/Documents/Generation_to_Generation_Gauging_the_Golden_Years.pdf.

shared with me what they would do if they were in charge of things. Some had a list. They had new rules they'd implement. These ranged from "Everybody should be nice to everybody" to "You should have to wear a Pokémon shirt on Mondays." They had great things they would accomplish, like space travel, circus performing, and, one of my favorites, "taking the pictures of hamburgers that you see on menus." Still others seemed to dread the day it'd be their turn. As a fifth grader memorably wrote to me, "I don't want to grow up because then you have to clean up all the throw up."

One student's description of being a grownup earned a spot above my desk. I grabbed a thumbtack and stuck it there because something about it really spoke to me. Using colored pencils, he'd drawn a stick figure standing beside a car. Above this he'd written:

"YOU HAVE A BIG RESPOSABLETY AND YOU CAN DO WHAT EVER YOU WANT."

This was like one of those great motivational posters you'd see in an office or a classroom. Except this didn't have a cat dangling from a limb with the words "Hang in there," nor was it an eagle in flight with inspiring words about soaring or success. It was a scrappy little stick person standing next to a modestly drawn vehicle with a mixed message of blessing and burden. It was like this kid was giving me a reminder, but also permission. You can do whatever you want! He'd totally captured the freedom. You have a big responsibility. He'd also captured the weight. It's burdens and blessings and it's balancing it all. Yes, you can do whatever you want, but there's also dishes to be done and throw up to be cleaned up.

I'd become more and more interested in seeing what older people had chosen to do with this freedom and responsibility. It came out of a budding curiosity and a deep need to see what I, myself, might be marching toward. It seemed to me more and more that aging was walking away from so many youthful things I'd held dear. As I put together my list, I worked to include men and women who'd grown up but still somehow held on to a childlike exuberance. One of these was a man I'd admired for a long time.

Michael is a storyteller and teacher who has, for decades, collected narratives from different cultures all over the world. I'd been encouraged by him for a long while and was interested in spending more time trying to understand how he thought about things. Recently, he'd been using his gifts to help young people dealing with depression, addiction, and anxiety. I knew there was a lot I could learn from his mentorship programs and classes, but I also knew deep down that being with him would be illuminating. Michael delivered immediately:

"Everybody is getting older. That's not an accomplishment. The trick is to get *elder*."

He'd seen many of his friends age. Of those, he explained, some had become better, some bitter, and some had morphed into what he described as "dangerous, angry children in grownup skin." These were all versions of older people I'd known and seen. I'd also imagined myself growing into each of those various roles. Maybe one day I'd become a truly great old man who gave out candy and wisdom to every person he met. I could also see how dashed dreams and disappointments could, over time, fashion me into a closed-off curmudgeon. Becoming a dangerous, angry child in grownup skin was certainly not one of my goals, though. Thankfully, he pointed me toward something hopeful and truly aspirational.

There is a way to step into adulthood with awe and beauty. Michael shared with me what he's learned about aging from his friend Malidoma Patrice Somé. Malidoma is an elder in the West African Dagara tribe. In this tradition, becoming an official elder of the tribe is not something you declare yourself. That's not behavior befitting of an elder. Nor is it something you can campaign for. A true elder wouldn't create promotional signs, bumper stickers, or Instagram posts. Being an elder is something you embody. You are then tapped on the shoulder when the time comes and asked to serve. There is even a song the tribe sings, which is a "call for elders." It cries out that many of the oldest among them have died. *Azi so na. Eze ma culi. Azi so na. Te semani. Ba de na.* This translates roughly to "The world has gone wrong. Somebody take us home. The world has gone wrong. We're losing our fathers." It is an announcement that there is a great need. The time has come for those who are of age to accept responsibility not just for themselves but also for the direction of the entire tribe. Rise up, elders! Rise up!

As he described this to me, he softly sang the words of the song. I could feel every hair on my arms stand on end. The song holds a great sadness for the state of things but also a great hope for those who might accept the responsibility to lead everyone forward. This urgent plea would surely be delivered with a painful lump in each singer's throat. It acknowledges all that is being lost around them while at the same time dreaming about what could be. This rallying cry seemed to articulate a deep-seated feeling I'd had within me but did not have the words for.

This is so vastly different from the way we handle aging in U.S. culture. I wondered how a call for elders might go over in my neighborhood. As someone who'd spent the last two years listening to children, I'd become more aware than ever of the deep need for loving grownups in every corner of the world. This was, finally, something challenging and exciting to march toward. Also, as a current grownup in progress, I, too, could use some older, wiser guides to rise up. Could I stand on my lawn and sing this song or maybe put an ad in the paper?

Our culture is pretty good at creating *olders*, but we don't necessarily excel at raising up *elders*. I didn't realize it when I started, but I think that was the impetus for this book. Sure, I felt unworthy of being called a grownup, but honestly, I didn't really want to become one. I had no interest in getting older. Becoming a grownup meant I was a step closer to death. Maybe we need more people tapping us on the shoulders and inviting us into life, getting *elder*. That's a journey I can be excited about.

There really aren't any moments in our culture when we intentionally invite people to rise up. We have elections. We have graduations, birthday celebrations, and other moments when we mark a transition. Rarely, though, do we tell people in our community that we need their specific gifts and experience to be used in shaping and guiding the younger people around them.

It's a big responsibility, and you can do whatever you want.

One of my favorite examples of seeing this kind of grownup began in a Boston, Massachusetts, classroom. The teacher, Catherine Epstein, discovered something troubling. She'd been struck by the way people online talked about those who were different from themselves, especially when it came to politics. Like many people, she'd grown tired of cable news and heated debates on social media. She originally thought these generalizations came only from more closed-minded people—you know, former kids, *olders*. However, she began to recognize that her young students were also already very interested in what was happening in the news. She noticed they, too, had similar ideas about current events and weren't shy about sharing them. However, they did all seem to have similar takes and seemed to be very unaware of how anyone could ever see things differently.

Seeing the vitriol of public discourse all over the world and already noticing the seeds of it in her young students, she decided to do something. Catherine might not be able to change the whole world, but she could at least change her classroom. So that's what she did. She started a pen pal program. The idea was to connect her city-dwelling, largely left-leaning students with a group of kids in a very different environment. She found a classroom in Ozark, Arkansas, in what was described by their teacher, Cherese, as a "very rural, ultra-conservative public school."

It's not often that you start a relationship based on disagreement, but this experiment would challenge a lot about what they knew relationships to be. With this project, Catherine and her new, very different friend Cherese set out to show their students what it could look like to disagree beautifully—a course many grownups in the world could use. For me, following their journey changed the way I view friendships, disagreements, and connection forever.

Between the two schools, there was already the massive difference of place. As Catherine put it, "Just what they see outside their windows is different." Beyond their geography, the way they view themselves and their happenings in it were drastically different, too. Catherine and Cherese set out to help guide their students through the many differences. They let them know who'd they be writing to. Each group immediately had assumptions about the other as the letter writing began. Off they went.

The first few months, students got to know one another. These letters were mini-biographies mixed with questions for their new, mostly unknown friends. They shared information about their communities and their homes, hobbies, and families. Many included drawings and details beyond the scope of what was asked—in doing so, adding human flourishes to what was, essentially, just a school project. The old-fashioned act of actually writing a letter was new to the students. It was a slower way of connecting than they were used to, causing them to reflect on their thoughts and making the letters a personal exploration as much as a cultural connection.

Both classes would wait eagerly for each new batch of letters. They became a key that unlocked conversations the students didn't know they wanted to have and caused them to find words and feelings they didn't know were inside them. As the letters progressed, students began confronting differences with prompts from their teachers. Difficult and divisive topics like race, religion, gender, and guns were incorporated into the discussions. These were the sorts of topics you might not want to talk about around a dinner table with immediate family, much less with strangers via letter. Yet they did. With their teachers as their guides, the students explored how to share and how to listen.

It took some work to find the right words, though. The two teachers felt their role was to show the students how to use what they called "helpful" words. The work became very much about creating constructive conversations, which meant that the students were not focused on proving themselves correct, being especially clever, or trying to convert their new friends to their perspective. Even with their own differences, these two educators formed a friendship based on their trust that this pen pal project would help their students gain a better understanding of themselves and people they disagreed with.

The project started out wonderfully, but something they didn't plan for began to happen. When conversations became slightly heavy or seemed to be moving into a space that might threaten the warm, friendly nature of their earlier letters, the students would pull back. They'd return to discussing less divisive things like music and classwork and the weather. When I heard about this, I found it charming. Even with their strongly held beliefs and opinions, these students felt a very human need to preserve their new friendships. They longed for peace, and I found that beautiful and hopeful.

The teachers, though, were wiser than me and realized this wasn't actually helping the students grow. They were no longer stretching or challenging their ideas. They were holding back. This would not result in developing empathy for someone who might see things differently. Instead, they were just ignoring their differences.

Uncomfortable as it might be, these teachers realized they'd need to push their students beyond avoidance. For most of their young lives, the examples they'd been shown of handling conflict were aggressive. They were examples of people attacking one another. The only other example they'd been shown was avoidance, which is what they'd all started emulating.

So these teachers and guides showed them a different way.

Catherine invited a friend to her class named John, an expert in disputes. To be clear, John doesn't cause disputes but rather helps create conversations and resolutions around them. His team, Essential Partners, works to help people navigate conflict. To do that, they help people realize that we're all essential partners in this life. The idea is to see the humanity in other people and engage with it. The key, he revealed to the students, was being clear that this was about *investigation*. Calling it an *investigation* helped frame the conversation for students in a way that allowed them to hang on to their friendships while also engaging with their differences.

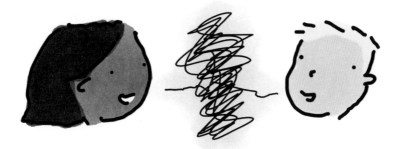

Surprisingly, John's approach wasn't about finding common ground or persuading or even agreeing. It was about having genuine interest in each other. Each student would have to speak about where they were coming from and each student would agree that all other students were essential teammates on this planet with them. Seeing the humanity and engaging with it was the goal.

I got to spend some time with Catherine's students. The effect the project had on them was visible almost immediately in how they interacted with me. It's remarkable what can happen when you treat someone as "essential," even if they're just a strange guy doing a listening tour. They reflected on how the letter writing changed them along the way. One student told me, "I used to think of people as 'other people' or as 'people that are wrong,' but now I can talk to them. Now I see everyone as a person worth listening to." The stories they'd believed about those who were different from them had been dismantled. Now they encountered real humans, with all their humanity, and couldn't see them otherwise. Even if they disagreed.

They opened up about earlier assumptions they'd had and were often embarrassed at how small their eyes had been. There's great humility required in admitting that. The students spoke of walking out of their classroom now feeling more accepting of oth-

ers. It was the kind of feeling I want for my own children. It's the sort of thing I want the whole world to know. I began to wish every human on the planet could somehow find themselves studying at the feet of Catherine and Cherese, two people embodying the role of *elders* right where they are, helping those in their midst find the humanity in everyone.

Thankfully, though, there are already teachers and guides, *elders*—not *olders*—all around us. People who are quietly and boldly showing the way forward. There's no magic age when you step into this role. I found that many *elders* I've met are not, in fact, elderly. These are just people recognizing a need where they are and doing what they can to rise up to meet it. These people are not campaigning. These people are not trying to acquire power. They are simply rising up to help others rise.

During my time with Michael, I asked him what sorts of things he, as someone working to get *elder* and not *older*, tells young people. Many of the kids he works with have either attempted to take their own lives or are at great risk of doing so. He told me, "The amount of suicide amongst young people is partially because they think they're worthless." This overwhelming sense of worthlessness cannot be conquered without deep, meaningful relationships. So he begins by making certain they know this:

"The first thing I always say: 'You don't have to become someone; you already are someone.'"

As he said this, an unexpected wave of emotion came over me. I couldn't explain it in that very moment, and I still struggle to understand it all. Somehow he'd

tapped into wounds I hadn't realized I'd been carrying around. My eyes filled with tears. His healing words were exactly what I needed. *You already are someone.* An avalanche of internet comments over the past few years had made me feel otherwise. The sneaking suspicion that I needed to accomplish something spectacular to be worth anything had left me exhausted. The treadmill of trying to be more had left me feeling less than enough. For so long I'd believed that I wasn't up to the task of becoming a good grownup, much less the better grownup I wanted to be for myself and my kids. Yet I was already someone of value.

Hearing an adult I respected say these words was the moment I finally started to believe them.

I'd walked into the party that everyone called "adulthood" and didn't know where to set my stuff. Awkwardly, I'd entered into this stage of life still carrying a backpack, bumbling around with a bag filled with so many things I'd thought I would easily outgrow. My insecurities were in there, as were my fears. There were stories being lugged around in that backpack—heavy stories, many of them untrue. Yet I'd been carrying that bulky thing everywhere, and it'd been weighing me down. A weight lifted.

There's a Latin phrase, *sum quod eris*, which means "I am what you will be." You can imagine a mentor saying this to an apprentice, or a parent saying it to a child. In some ways, this is said as aspirational: *I am what you might one day become.* This could also very easily be read as a threat. *DO YOU SEE ME? This is what you're becoming. This is where you're headed. I AM WHAT YOU WILL BE!* Initiate child's nightmare mode.

This is not how *elders* lead. Yes, they are great examples and role models. However, better grownups aren't on a mission to create duplicates of themselves. As I see it, a better grownup looks younger people in the eyes and tells them they're already a vital note in the symphony. They're waking people up to the irreplace-

BACKPACK I CARRIED for WAY TOO LONG

able miracle they are and to the irreplaceable miracle everyone around them is.

The image of adulthood in media (and in children's artwork) is often unflattering. Parents on children's shows are the butts of jokes. The grownups are portrayed as bumbling, dull, or emotionless. These images aren't far off from those big, busy, and boring portraits of adults that kids had presented me with throughout the Listening Tour. The world might be crowded with poor models of adulthood—childish people stuck where they are, begging for power or attention. It's a big responsibility, and you can do whatever you want. There are, though, many—like Michael, Catherine, and Cherese—who are quietly, daily answering the call to rise up and lead.

If you pay attention, you can hear it. Listen closely and you'll begin to notice the urgent call for *elders* that's being sung daily. It comes in whispers and shouts. It comes from kids and former kids, some carrying backpacks they should've checked at the door long ago. The call can be heard in the healing words of mentors, guides, and loved ones all around. Maybe, also, if we open our eyes, we'll begin to see it, too. We'll see true images of what it looks like to grow *elder*. We'll start to recognize our *elders*, celebrate them, listen to them. And year by year, wrinkle by wrinkle, step by step, we'll cheerfully become them.

CHAPTER TWELVE

THE WONDER SOCIETY

Recently my wife texted me a picture of our kids. She was out with them at the grocery store, and the photo showed them standing and pointing with their eyes wide and their mouths open. You could sense the excitement. She then sent this text: "What do you think our kids are looking at?"

I responded with a question mark. She sent another photo. In it, the kids are standing in the exact same spot, but their eyes are even wider. Both our son and daughter appear to be squealing with delight.

She then asked me again: "What do you think our kids are looking at?"

This time I responded with multiple question marks and a confused-looking emoji. "What? What? I'm dying to know!"

She sent yet another photo. Even amid all the pointing and screaming, my wife had somehow been able to take multiple photos of our kids standing in the same spot. This was, in itself, a kind of parenting miracle. The kids continued to be frozen in wonder.

What were they looking at? What had captured their imaginations so fully?

What had come into their lives and transfixed them to such a massive degree? A cardboard display for soda, of course. Really. It was just a large cardboard man and in his hand was a soda can. The can was mounted on little springs, making it move back and forth. That's it.

I know you're thinking, *These people should take their kids out more*. Yet if you've spent even just a little time around children recently, you'll know that kids find joy in things we grownups might ignore. They play with boxes instead of the presents inside the boxes. They like the bubble wrap more than the expensive toy that the bubble wrap was protecting. They just see things differently than we do. Part of this has to do with their height, sure. How hideous we must look from their perspective! Have you ever accidentally reversed the camera of your cellphone and gotten a picture looking directly up your nose? Well, that's about the vantage point many kids have of our faces. No wonder they have such mixed ideas about growing up.

Still, we'd do well to look at the world with childlike eyes. My children and all the kids I met

along the Listening Tour possess uncanny abilities to see things in ways I'd forgotten. It's a way of looking at the world with eyes full of radical amazement. For children, the quest for wonder isn't so much a search but a zip code in which they already live. From there, they see everything. Clouds, crunching leaves, textures of blankets—all opportunities to sit in awe. Educator Walt Streightiff said, "There are no seven wonders in the eye of a child. There are seven million."

This way of seeing the world was something I'd expected to find in kids. Yet as I began interviewing people who were much older, I discovered something surprising and enlightening. For some of these people it'd been many decades since they were children. Some of them were now in nursing homes or retirement facilities. Though they'd outgrown so much, these better grownups had held on to something from childhood and they weren't letting go: eyes full of wonder.

At the age of 102, Mrs. Frances Hesselbein might very well be the youngest oldest person I've ever met. I share with you her age for the purpose of giving you and myself something wonderful to *work backward* toward. She told me that women love to ask her age. "Men never dare!" she said.

But when asked, her response is masterful: "I smile sweetly and say, 'May I quote my grandfather?' And they say, 'Oh sure, please!' And then I tell them, 'My grandfather always said [*now shouting*], "Age is irrelevant! It is what you do with your life that counts!"'" This quieted them.

Mrs. Hesselbein always spoke with a mischievous gleam in her eyes. Even her saying "Hello, Brad!" made it sound like she was up to something. That's because she's always been up to something. She served as CEO of the Girl Scouts from 1976 to 1990. During that time, the number of young girls involved in the program went from being in decline to hitting more than two million active and

FRANCES HESSELBEIN
(leader, servant, door opener,
amazing grownup)

passionate leaders in training. Plus, she was able to equip and empower more than seven hundred thousand adult volunteers to walk alongside these young women. She was awarded the Presidential Medal of Freedom by Bill Clinton in 1998. When introducing her, he made sure to mention her disapproval of "hierarchical words like *up* and *down*," so he invited her to come not up, but instead to come *forward* to receive her recognition.

When the two of us spoke, she made no mention of receiving this honor, nor did she list qualifications off her résumé.

Her love of words like *forward* did come up a lot, though. As someone in a leadership position, she realized early on that the language used in organizations was too often about moving up or falling down. There were superiors and inferiors. "I wanted everyone to be together in a circle," she said. "Equal and growing together. Going forward together."

"Circles, like around a campfire?" I asked.

"Yes! Around the warmth of a fire! What a circle! And oh, how we grow in circles."

This woman was not the image of *old* that many might think of. Yes, her body movements were slow. Her speech and steps were carefully calculated. Yet these

we grow in circles.
— FRANCES HESSELBEIN

were not hindrances but just little details. Physical cues revealed that she'd had a few more birthdays than I had, but that's it. Her vibrant enthusiasm, passion, and purpose eclipsed any physical signs of aging. It's a spirit you might call youthful, or maybe *elder*. Undeniably, she was fully alive.

"Mrs. Hesselbein," I whispered, as if we were kids in a tree fort, "what's the secret?" I leaned in as I asked and eagerly awaited her response. Maybe she'd recommend a skin cream or prescribe me some specific diet. I wondered if there was a series of books I'd need to go through. Maybe a fountain somewhere I could visit and dip my face in every summer solstice. What was her secret to aging with such grit and grace?

She whispered back to me, playfully but earnestly: "To serve is to live.

"To serve is to live!" she repeated, louder this time. "You look to where you can serve. Where can you make a difference? It's not a secret. I'll say it loudly."

This had been her battle cry. Looking back at all she'd accomplished, and at all she continued to accomplish, I realized that service really was a guiding principle throughout her life. "To be a good grownup means that we care about all people," she told me. "It's not just about yourself." For more than a century now, she'd been on this planet and had used her time in service to others. Her eyes lit up as she detailed story after story.

It was the same wide-eyed spark I'd seen when I spoke with children. It was the same glimmer I'd continue to see in the eyes of all those grownups who'd held on to their childlike wonder. It was the wonder I'd seen in Walker's eyes when he talked to me about the chapters of life. In our conversations, he'd warned me that life could contain regret or rejoicing. In my conversations with senior citizens I met, their eyes showed both.

Like Eugene. He's ninety-two and in a retirement home. We'd initially connected over a game of checkers and continued our conversation into the afternoon. He was reserved but kind. Most of his answers were short, but one was especially so. When I asked him if he had any regrets, he responded:

"I should've called her back."

That's it. That's literally all of the story he would share. He tried to repeat the sentence, but couldn't complete it the second time. Too much pain. We'd only just met, and everything else in our conversation had been light and somewhat joyful. But that—that sentence came from a deep reservoir of regret. I didn't push him for more details. His eyes told me enough.

He hugged me as we said our goodbyes, even though he didn't seem like the type to do so. I thanked him for his time and his honesty and also assured him that he'd inspired me to love the people around me while I can. The corners of his mouth turned to a smile, and I could still spot a little light in his eyes.

The things we do have consequences. The same is also true for the things we don't do. My new friend Mrs. Hesselbein had regrets, but she told me that they're "few and far between." She said the key is to "learn from the past, dream about the future, but keep focused on looking around you for who you can serve *now*." It was a perspective that seemed childlike at first in its simplicity, yet was rooted in deep wisdom and experience. Almost as if she'd found a way to grow and move forward in life without losing that youthful spark.

I've always loved the story of Peter Pan. The idea of a boy who never grows up is fascinating. Since J. M. Barrie introduced the character and the idea, it has captured imaginations all over the world. He's the embodiment of what it means to rebel against adulthood. To stick it to the grownups. This story has been told and retold, and often, in many ways, lived.

While the idea of never growing up might make a good story, the image of a grown man in green tights wandering through the woods or popping into bedroom windows is unsettling. There's even a syndrome named after it. Psychologist Dan Kiley used the term *Peter Pan syndrome* in the 1970s to describe the behavior of an adult who does not mature socially. In real life there's nothing adventurous about getting stalled in adolescence. The image of someone never growing into the person they're meant to become—well, there's a sadness to it.

But what if instead of celebrating *Peter Pan, or The Boy Who Wouldn't Grow Up*, we flipped the story and told it as *Wendy, or The Girl Who Grew Up*?

I think the story of Wendy is where the real adventure is. It's about a child who, like all children,

"All children, except one, grow up."
— J. M. Barrie, Peter Pan

has great courage, compassion, and creativity. In this story, dear young Wendy is told by her father that it is time to leave the nursery. She will move from the comfort of the gentle place she has known her entire life and into a room of her own. Frightened and unable to sleep on the eve of knowing she must grow up, Wendy imagines a far-off world where she'll never have to.

This Neverland is a world of her own making. There's flying by starlight. Danger lurks at every corner. She soars with Peter Pan alongside her younger siblings. She's brought them along, because even in the midst of such imaginative play, she can't help remaining the caring sister. It is just who she is and who she's becoming.

She delights in the idea of never growing up but throughout Neverland sees needs all around her: for a teacher, caregiver, storyteller, and guide. In this world, she finds rivalry and struggle, envy and violence. Innocence is threatened by the grownups who sail

this world as pirates. The lost boys of Neverland are kids who've refused to grow up. Though she herself is scrappy and uninterested in leaving childhood behind, she looks at the rough-and-tumble Lost Boys and their leader, Peter Pan. She feels a deep sadness. Wendy determines to become neither pirate nor lost child. She decides that growing up would be the greatest adventure of all.

I think the best story would be a young girl who visited Neverland, bravely returned home, and never forgot it. We don't need more Peter Pans. We need more Wendys. We need people who've flown, tasted magic, and dedicated themselves to carrying that wonder with them everywhere they go.

I get why Peter Pan stays in Neverland. But the real hero is Wendy. Though she wants to stay in the comfort of what she knows, she chooses growth. What if our culture celebrated the story of an inventive girl who is so brave and has so much moxie that she does the boldest thing of all: grows up? And what if this brilliant girl grows into a young woman who holds on to her imagination, even as the rest of the world tries to quiet it?

We can choose to remain stuck like Peter Pan. We can choose to remain suspended, stalled, scared children fearfully clinging to what we know. But wouldn't it be more exciting to embrace an innocent openness to whatever might be next? Hanging on to the imagination you've had from the very beginning, yet growing in wisdom. Showing the world what can happen when a child grows into adulthood and yet somehow doesn't forget the magic of growth. That's the brave thing.

My 102-year-old friend Mrs. Frances Hesselbein regularly paused during our time together to grab my hand. She'd just smile and say, "Wow. We're here!" Little interruptions to wake us both up to the wonder. Radical amazement at the simple fact that we were together. Maybe that's something you start to realize once you've been alive for so many years. It's a miracle we're here. You start speaking

like someone giving an acceptance speech at the Academy Awards, full of gratitude and realizing you don't have much time.

Frances loves Ralph Waldo Emerson. "He said in 1847, 'Be ye an opener of doors,' and it is as relevant today as it was then," she told me. "We open doors for ourselves, but we also open doors for other people. We're all partners together on this marvelous journey."

This marvelous journey, indeed. Better grownups open doors of possibility. They invite others into new ways of seeing. My ideas about aging were changing. For so long, I'd placed a wall between myself and older people. I'd believed I belonged forever at the kids' table. Frances shattered that notion, or more aptly—she opened a door. She welcomed me to a circle. There I could see her humanity, and she could see mine. To me, respecting my elders meant leaving them alone. Peter Pan was whom I looked to. Now I want to be more like Wendy or maybe more like Frances, walking and flying with wisdom and wonder.

"be ye an opener of doors!"

It was just an ordinary Tuesday when we spoke. Just another interview for my listening project. As we wrapped up, she told me, "Now you're part of my story, and I'm part of your story! Isn't that remarkable?" It is. It is remarkable. When we take time to see life with childlike wonder, we are reminded how life is relentlessly remarkable. I used to think life was relentless and occasionally remarkable, but now I know better. Each day we're presented with an unending parade of wonders, should we not be too busy to notice. Even in the face of pain and difficulty, we can know we stand in the midst of something absolutely, completely, relentlessly remarkable. People, young and old, who live in radical amazement open us up to seeing more—souls in human bodies on a rotating rock in a universe held together by love. Or we could just call it Tuesday.

Our weird little lives are spent traveling on a ball around the sun, and somehow we act like this is normal. In all the *everydayness* of life, we forget the *everythingness* of life. Somehow the youngest and oldest among us already know this. We miss out on reasons to point and scream and laugh like my kids do. Noticing the immense beauty of each moment is something I don't want to outgrow, though in many ways I already have. Thankfully, there are reminders all around us.

I've now heard so many children tell me what they want to do when they grow up. Hearing their responses, I know that only a fraction of them will actually follow through with it. I've seen what happens. We outgrow certain ideas and attitudes. Sometimes because they're childish or preposterous. But too often, fears, uncertainties, or regrets cloud once wonder-filled eyes. Someone tells us we can't do something and we believe them.

I want to be a nurse and help people.
— LILY, AGE 9

I want to eat ice cream and that is all. I just want to eat ice cream.
— SAM, AGE 8

I want to live on the sun.
— RILEY, AGE 8

The more time I spent around children and the elderly, the more I began to recognize my own childishness. I'd dropped my backpack but hung on to so many things I should've outgrown, while at the same time I'd outgrown so many things I should've held on to. The trick is to trade in our childishness for things that are more childlike. To trade in our childish *fear* and in return receive childlike *fascination*. To exchange impatient tantrums for joyful tippy-toe dances no matter the circumstances. Selfishness for generosity. Busyness for bliss. It's all about living with eyes full of wonder, like a child.

CHILDISH → CHILDLIKE

SELFISH → GENEROUS

ENTITLED → COMPASSIONATE

FEARFUL → FASCINATED

CLOSED OFF → OPEN

FRUSTRATED → FREE

ANGERED → AMAZED

BUSY → BLISSFUL

I used to carry a business card. I thought this was what you were supposed to do when you were a grownup. I'm not going to lie: I did feel pretty grownup when they came in the mail. Still, though, I felt like I was playing the part of a grownup. Handing them out never really led to a deeper connection. It was just a transfer of contact information. So I pitched them.

I made an entirely new card. It has very little information on it. Whenever I meet someone on a plane or at a business meeting, or anytime people are trading contact info, I carefully hand them the card. I let them know it's their induction into the Wonder Society. I tell them to sign their name. Now they're in my secret club.

Mrs. Hesselbein is in the Wonder Society, of course. So is every kid I met during my travels, as well as every elder. You can be a card-carrying member, too, though it doesn't require a card. All it takes is opening your eyes. Be dedicated to wonder—see it, create it, and share it.

My son and I were going to the grocery store. He was in his car seat, and I looked in the rearview mirror to notice he had made circles with his thumb and index fingers placed over each eye like binoculars. I asked him what he was doing. He told me they were his "adventure goggles." I guess one can never be too careful when going to the grocery store.

I decided to take his lead. With hand binoculars over our eyes, we marched through the store together like explorers. This grocery store was a place I'd been

PUT YOUR ADVENTURE GOGGLES ON!

many times before, but now it was entirely new. Surely, it looked ridiculous, a grown man and a toddler playing pretend down each aisle. It was worth it, though, to hear my son's laugh. It was worth it, too, for me to see such a normal outing through his bright, unclouded eyes.

While at the register, I could tell the cashier was curious, so I explained what we were doing. I held out my hands and pretended to give her a pair of adventure goggles. My son couldn't believe it when he looked up and saw her hands over her eyes, too. "Wow," she said.

I know. Wow.

CHAPTER THIRTEEN

SONGS THAT
TIME FORGOT

There's some sort of magic that makes tin-can phones work. I've looked up the specifics, and, intellectually, I get it. Vibrations from our voices travel through the can and on to the string. It's sound waves rippling from one can to another. This is, I'm told, just simple science. There's nothing special about the can or the string. But still, there's just something about holding a soup can, speaking into it, and having your voice flutter across string that can only be described as magic.

When we started making *Kid President* videos, I mailed out old soup cans to celebrities. These had bright strands of yarn attached with a note included. In the note I explained that this was a magic can phone and was the only official way to connect to the tiny president of the universe. They would have to use this can if they wanted to chat with us. Looking back, I realize these recipients had every reason to dismiss these odd packages altogether. Yet they believed in the magic. Confession: I started all this and, well, I still can't believe it worked.

These notes and tin cans connected us to people like Michelle Obama, Steve Martin,

Jamie Foxx, and Beyoncé. I found that whether someone was a First Lady, a legend of comedy, an Academy Award–winning actor, or a singer-songwriter who could sell millions of albums and fill a stadium, they all seemed charmed to get to play. They'd each smile as they held the old soup cans with yarn. So often they'd remark on how much they'd loved making can phones and playing with them as kids.

I was stunned. Not only that words can travel through air by way of twisted yarn, but also that this idea had worked at all. Even though I'd sent the cans out in the hope that people would respond, I never imagined it'd work as well as it did. From my small town in rural Tennessee, I connected with cultural icons, heroes, and legends, and the list only continued to grow. Somehow my little words and little cans found their way across states and sometimes even borders and oceans.

Just before sending out that very first can phone, I was working in a job I enjoyed. It was safe and I was happy. My notebooks, though, were packed with ideas I'd rather be doing. There were short films I'd been wanting to make and stories I'd been wanting to tell. One weekend I started talking about one of my ideas when a friend interrupted me. He said something that at first made me mad, then moved me to action, and now I am forever grateful for:

"You are so creative. You have so many great ideas, but we're all just waiting to see if you're ever going to actually do one of them."

Boom. There it was. The end of our friendship.

No, actually his words were the provocation I needed. He was right, so I set out to show him. I began committing myself to following through on ideas and not just talking about them. *Kid President* and mailing out can phones was one of those ideas. Yet proving someone wrong wasn't my only motivation. Deep down, I had so much I wanted to share with the world about joy and hope but had been too fearful to do so. Since elementary school, I'd had that persistent feeling of wanting to share, but I'd allowed fear to hold me back. During those days, it was my fourth-grade teacher who gave me the confidence. Because of her, I started drawing comics for the school newspaper. Now I was again feeling that confidence slip. Sharing what's in your heart can be scary.

Whoever said, "You're your own worst critic," never posted anything on the internet. Everyone tells you not to read the comments, but of course I did. You're also told not to let the negative ones get to you, but of course I did that, too. With each new video, I'd lose myself in worry over how it might be received. Even when the majority of the feedback would be overwhelmingly positive, my silly brain would allow me to hear only the destructive comments.

With the Listening Tour, I began mailing can phones out again. These were for classroom visits happening through video calls. And the kids reacted with the same glee as the celebrities. I'd be on the other end holding my can and string, feigning an inability to hear them if they didn't speak into the can. Most kids loved when it was their turn to hold the can. Still, though, some kids were painfully shy and needed a little extra encouragement from their teacher and classmates. When the tension cooled, these silences would break. Without fail, these shy students would share something breathtaking.

I understood the shy voices most of all. With their voices shaking, these kids shared anyway. Surely their thoughts were flashing through all the things people had said to them or about them. They were doing a bit of preemptive editing, deciding what would be appropriate or inappropriate to share. If only they knew how valuable all they have to share is. If only everyone knew. If only I knew.

I've always loved musicals. I love how intense feelings that are normally kept inside suddenly come bursting out in a song. Characters in a musical tap into their innermost longings and share them with perfect clarity and harmony. They all somehow find a way to give voice to the truest things inside them. Mermaids reveal how they want to be where the people are. Little lions pounce and declare how much they want to be king. Murderous women express their desire to turn adorable puppies into luxury fur coats. Everybody sings their song.

Taking part in a project where I just stopped and listened was like hearing little portions of a much larger piece of music.

Whether it was retirees or elementary students, they were all in their spots adding their individual notes. I began to see every person as a player in a mighty orchestra. Right on cue and right in tune, the beauty of their individual contributions rivaled those of any of history's great musicians. Though each was so different in their tones and sounds, I remained in complete awe at the unexpected harmony I discovered.

For a long time I believed I was just a misfit fated to forever play out of tune. There were tons of things I'd written and created that I'd never shared. When I shared a portion of my voice with *Kid President*, I remained terrified that the world would not want to hear anything else I had to offer. Ever.

It was the voice of a much older person who helped me understand how wrong it was to silence my own. Her name was Martha. My friend Taylor had met her at a local rehabilitation facility. He's a filmmaker and is the kind of guy who loves people. Because of that, he's always uncovering fascinating stories. From love stories to tragedies, from magicians to heavyweight boxers, he somehow finds a way to notice and celebrate the humanity in every person.

Following a series of health issues, Martha had begun an extended stay in this facility. When not resting and recovering, she had been spending her time playing piano. Martha would sit in the community area and play whatever her heart desired. During

meals, she could often be found there, filling the space with her music. Many would gather around the piano; some would make song requests. One man, there with his wife who had Alzheimer's, would regularly ask for a song that was very special to the two of them. It was *their* song. Hearing it was medicine to them. Playing it was medicine to Martha.

It was an unlikely meeting. Taylor's mom was visiting a friend who'd been in a car accident. During her visits, in addition to the sounds of other people conversing and eating, she also overheard the soft tones of someone playing piano, someone she came to know as Martha.

Taylor took his mom's advice and met up with Martha. There, seated at the piano with her fingers on the keys, she became, he discovered, a treasured friend. In their conversations, he learned that at age five she'd started playing piano, and it was clearly the place where she felt most at home. He also discovered that she'd written stacks and stacks of songs. She'd long had a dream of writing and recording songs for children. She said she'd always hoped to get them published, at the very least just for her grandchildren to hear.

Martha shared songs with Taylor that she'd carried with her for so many years. As she did, Taylor wished there were more people in the room to hear them. These were bright, happy songs that he couldn't believe had been hidden. Now he knew what he had to do. These once buried songs needed to be out in the world for others to hear—especially for her grandchildren to hear. It was finally time for Martha to share.

They say necessity is the mother of invention, but I really think it's a trio of love, hope, and joy. When you're sparked by a love for something or someone, you become innovative really quickly.

Solid brick walls can't stop you. There'll be holes shaped like Kool-Aid Man where you've busted through. Nothing can stop a song that must be heard. Taylor found a way.

He set up a studio, gathered some musician friends, and helped Martha record her songs. The entire process was an about-face from how either of them lived day-to-day. Taylor wasn't in the habit of visiting rehab facilities and scouting talent. And this was the first time Martha had any of her music or singing recorded. She giggled each time she spoke into the microphone, continually astounded that this was actually happening. These were new steps for everybody involved, but that's what it takes to put new music out into the world.

When I heard the songs, I could not stop smiling. They were cheerful and catchy and sweet. These songs reminded me of that great library of classic children's songs we'd all grown up with, except these were new. They sounded like they should've always existed but for some reason hadn't. Beyond the great songcraft, you could feel the joy radiating out of the recordings. In one of my favorite moments, you can hear Martha speaking on one of the tracks. She's raising and lowering her voice playfully so she can hear herself in the headphones. She goes up an octave too high and laughs at how funny it sounds. She then brings her voice down far too low and finds that funny, too. At the end of this, she jokingly says, "They're probably going to come ask me to join the symphony!" This really made her laugh.

A few months later, I started to wonder if we might explore other ways of having Martha's songs heard. Then, a friend invited me to speak at an event he was doing. It would be held—I couldn't believe it—at the Schermerhorn Symphony Center in Nashville, Tennessee. This architecturally gorgeous, historic, and beautiful music hall is where the world-famous Nashville Symphony performs. Now it would also be home to the premiere of an unheard song by the great Martha.

She had written one called "Going to the Fair" that I particularly loved. It's a cheerful little tune about—yep, you guessed it—going to the fair. It's the kind of song you can't sing without smiling and turning into a giant child. So I thought it'd be the perfect choice.

Next I needed some backup. I was afraid I'd get too nervous onstage or cry and just completely mess up the whole thing. So I invited a friend. Emily Arrow is a songwriter and musician who, like Martha, creates music for children. I recruited her to play ukulele and help with vocals if needed. There would be close to a thousand people in the audience. We were trying to keep it a secret and surprise her. All was on track to get Martha on that stage to experience the whole thing and have her music performed at the symphony. Everything was falling into place.

Then it fell apart.

Just a few days before the big event, I got a call. A series of health setbacks had made it impossible for Martha to go anywhere. Plan over. Record scratch.

Taylor went to see Martha. He didn't want her to be disappointed, but he also wanted her to know what we'd been dreaming up in order to honor her. He thought it might lift her spirits to know she and her voice had inspired something. He also knew it'd been something she'd long dreamed of: having her music performed in a

symphony hall. Her response was laughter and then more laughter. She finally said, "Glory be!"

We began devising an alternate plan.

I'll never forget the day. Onstage, I shared the story of these two friends, Taylor and Martha. Then everyone in the audience was presented with lyrics. I'd arranged them in a way that would be quick and easy for everyone to pick up on. Just before leading everyone in this hidden gem of a song about going to the fair, a video played. Martha wanted to send everyone a word of thanks, so Taylor had filmed it. Martha's voice at last filled the symphony hall. Through laughter she said, "I'm at the symphony! Glory be!" Everyone cheered.

In addition to gratitude, her message included a gift of advice: "Keep at it. Don't give up hope. Enjoy life. It'll all work out."

It'll all work out, indeed. Martha's song started. It wasn't her singing it at the symphony, but instead hundreds of people she'd never met. Though it was a joyous children's song, some of the audience found themselves crying. I think for the same reasons I, too, cried. There are unsung songs within everyone. Discovering we have something of value to share with the world can sometimes take a lifetime. Sometimes we need people around us to recognize the notes within us and pull the music out of us. Fear can shut us up or close us off. It's a tragic thought to imagine all the music humanity has missed out on because people didn't realize the value of their voice to the whole of us all. The entire room shook with the same joy and love that had prompted Martha to write songs in the first place.

Better grownups are committed to hearing the music in every person. They are keyed in to hearing the songs that lie beneath the noise and beyond the fear. They make certain it is shared. They find there are always songs to be sung and parties to be planned.

Occasionally afternoon walks in the summer as a kid would take my brother and me in the direction of a house we found scary. Old country roads have endless surprises around every corner, and this house was one of the most surprising. We'd get near it and stop cold.

"Do you hear him?" my brother would ask.

I'd pause. We'd listen cautiously.

"No, I don't thi—"

Then we'd hear it. The unmistakable sound of an old man singing to nobody. You could hear him before you could even see him. Looking back, I think that was the scariest part. He just sat on his porch swing and stared at us wide-eyed as he sang. I couldn't tell you what the old man was singing. My brother and I would run as fast as we could past his house, stopping only to catch our breath, each making sure the other was still alive.

Moms have a way of calming fears with the truth. When we told her about the scary man singing on his front porch, our mom grinned. He was someone she and Dad had known for a long time. She explained that he just liked singing to his flowers. He believed that would help them grow and blossom in ways they wouldn't otherwise. Mom found it charming. We found it terrifying.

Looking back, I sort of envy that old man on his porch. He didn't care what we thought. He just sang. He just wanted his flowers to grow and so he did whatever it took. He just sang.

One of the earliest things we pick up on as infants is the power of voice. Our screaming and crying can get things done. As we get older, we discover all the many other things we can make happen with our voices. We see that one voice can change an entire room.

By shouting in anger or speaking softly in love, rooms are brought down or lifted higher. With invitation or judgment, people can feel welcome or unworthy. We speak, we shout, and we hold things in. For better or worse, with just a few words, one person can alter everything around them—even you, even me. We use this power, abuse this power, and forget this power.

Once on an airplane I was seated beside an older woman who was reading a gardening magazine. I asked her if she had a garden of her own. She came to life as she told me about her Tommy Toe tomatoes, bell peppers, Armenian cucumbers, and many failed attempts at growing squash. She was so passionate and knowledgeable that I decided to ask her the question:

"This might sound a little odd, but I've heard that if you sing to plants it can help them grow. Is that true?"

She laughed. "No, no. You know, that's something I've certainly heard, but there's nothing to prove that it works. It's just one of those old folktales that's been passed down all these years."

"Ah, yeah. I figured."

But something told me I should push a bit more. Maybe it was the tone in her voice or the way she'd talked about her garden. It might've been her quiet laugh that revealed a bit of surprise as I brought it up. So I followed up with another question:

"But, do *you* ever, you know, like . . . sing to your plants?"

"Yes, all the time."

The two of us laughed. I imagined the old man from my childhood who sang on his porch would've found this funny, too. Maybe they've been singing for all these years not to help plants grow but because it somehow helped them personally. Maybe the image of seeing someone older sing for the simple joy of singing helped the kids on their street grow, too. Sometimes our songs heal and nourish in ways we never intended. The space between each one of us is a sacred space where so much can and does happen. It is fertile ground for life to grow. So whether it's connection by can phone, face-to-face, or stringing together written words into sentences, sing, sing, sing. Don't hide your note. Share those songs.

CHAPTER FOURTEEN

LITTLE NUDGES

I was minding my own business, but in third grade you have to expect the unexpected. One minute you're listening to the teacher, and then the next thing you know, a note lands on your desk. You open it. Someone likes you. *Oh no.* Moments later you're simply visiting the water fountain and then presented with more abrupt news. A tap on the shoulder. Someone doesn't like you. *Oh no.*

School was a minefield of information, and I believed all of it. The likes. The dislikes. I even believed the curious group of girls who congregated around a small paper creation. Only one of the girls could operate it at a time. I assumed she was the oracle and they were merely groupies. The world of girls was already a mystery to me, but here they were claiming the ability to tell the future.

I've come to learn that some kids in other parts of the country called them cootie catchers. Other names for this thing include chatterbox, whirlybird, salt cellar, *paku-paku*, and the pretty straightforward origami fortune-teller. I never knew what this thing on their hands was called. There was always a hushed silence when it would appear. With reverence like this around it, I never heard them use a name.

A group of girls pulled me into their orbit. Like a sorcerer, the girl with the paper on her hand held it out for all to see. She opened and closed it to a rhythm I didn't understand. She announced that this would tell my future. I attempted to act like this was normal.

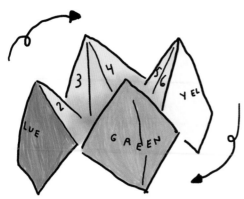

My wide eyes and open mouth surely gave me away as I, with deep fear, awaited my fate.

"Pick a color," she said.

"Blue," I responded.

Oh no. Why did I pick blue? More paper folds in and out. I am certain I have made a poor choice. I could've gone with yellow or red. Blake would've gone with red. Not me. I had to choose blue. Too late now, though. My destiny has already been decided. Except she presented me with another choice:

"Now, pick a number," she said.

"Five," I said.

"There's only one through four," all the girls said in unison.

I pick the number 3, and all their eyebrows go up. *Why did all their eyebrows go up? What do these girls know? Was I not supposed to pick 3? Have I already wrecked my entire life? Why did they have to decide my fate today? I'm leaving early to go to the dentist, and it's already a big day.*

She spoke: "You're going to drive . . . a green car . . ."

I can live with that, I think to myself.

". . . live . . . in a boat . . ."

Odd, but adventurous. This isn't so bad. Keep going . . .

". . . have seven kids . . ."

On a boat?

". . . and marry . . . Rachel."

I don't know Rachel very well, but . . .

Rachel's face told me that she was not excited about this prospect. More specifically, Rachel's face looked as if she'd just caught a glimpse of a dystopian future. She'd seen a *Hunger*

Games–Mad Max–Terminator mash-up of darkness that awaited her life to come. I wanted to console her, let her know that I'd do my best to make our future together happy. We could go for rides in my green car together. I'd even let her name all seven of the children. But, embarrassed, I walked away, hoping desperately that the future would somehow be better than that moment felt.

That little paper doodad was fake news. Things turned out better. Far better. I wish I could travel through time to let both Rachel and my younger self know that it all turns out okay. She doesn't have to marry me. I didn't get a green car or end up living on a boat. Those girls with that wad of paper didn't know what they were talking about. I wish I could somehow go back and plant a brighter vision of the future in all of those kids' heads. The future is bigger and better than anything you could fit on a piece of paper. That doesn't stop us from trying to predict what it might look like.

During the Listening Tour, I walked into one elementary school and noticed several photos on the wall. This was a project they'd done to celebrate the hundredth day of school. The students had imagined what it would look like and be like when they, themselves, turned one hundred years old. To make these predictions, students had their photos taken using an app that distorted their faces, making them appear several years older. This filter added wrinkles and lines, pulled their eyes down, and grayed their hair. Occasionally accessories were added, like bi-focals or old-timey hats. Below each image were thoughts from the students on what they would be like if they lived to be one hundred years old.

> *When I am one hundred years old, I will look and do things differently than I do now. I will walk very slow. I will make cookies for my grandkids. I will have very droopy cheeks.*

Then it ends with this:

> *I am looking forward to being one hundred years old.*

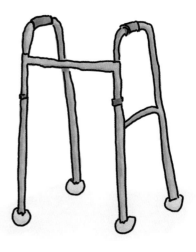

Really? Here's another:

> *When I am one hundred years old, I will have gray hair and dentures. I will be walking with a cane. I am going to live in a retirement home with my wife. I think turning one hundred will be amazing.*

It will be amazing. Or will it?

Lily Tomlin once said, "Wouldn't it be great if we all grew up to be what we wanted to be? The world would be full of nurses, firemen, and ballerinas." There's certainly the idea of what we'd all like to happen, and then there's the reality. These kids were play-fully blending their ideal future while also peppering in a few of the unwanted realities of aging. Based on what they've observed about getting older, kids know the future will likely include wrinkles and walkers. Hard candy and hearing loss. Kids sometimes mimic be-

coming older by arching their backs and putting their hands behind them to do so. They'll speak in slow, scratchy voices as they
act out what they think getting older might be.

None of these kids can predict what life will be like in the future. That definitely doesn't stop them or us from imagining what
things might be like. Through stories we make up and stories we
believe about what is to come in our own lives, we create visions
of the future. So often there can be a tendency to lean toward the
bleak. Many of the most popular stories about where humanity is
headed are dark. These are images of a world none of us want to
live in.

I think stories about dystopian futures are meant to move us
into action, to help us see the error of our ways. They're really just
entertainment, but somehow we've sort of started to believe them.

Our culture has stopped taking these dark ideas of what's to come as fiction and decided they are unavoidable. Like the destinies handed to us by the little girl in the back of the class with an all-seeing origami fortune-teller.

I discussed this very idea with an astronaut. Ron Garan was just a kid when he gathered with his family around a small black-and-white television set to watch as Apollo 11 landed on the moon. He was never the same, and decided to spend the rest of his life chasing after that dream. Since then he has spent more than 178 days in space and has traveled 71,075,867 miles in 2,842 orbits of our planet. In addition to his space missions, Ron has also served as an aquanaut, living and working in an underwater lab. It'd be easy to have a conversation with him and feel microscopic, given all that he's accomplished. That's not how he operates, though. Ron sees things with different eyes—adventure goggles.

Many astronauts return to Earth with stories of how they view life differently. It's become known as the *overview effect*. Being detached from everything they'd ever known and experienced and then finding themselves looking down at their home planet has profoundly affected several of our explorers in space. For Ron, his moment came as he dangled outside the International Space Station and looked to see the beauty of Earth 240 miles below him. He was moved by the beauty—and also struck by the inequity. Below him was a planet with everything it needed for those who inhabited it, yet they were unable to see themselves as a human family.

When I first spoke with Ron, it was of course through can and string. This man is one of the most decorated pilots; he is a brilliant researcher and a daring explorer. On that day, though, I had to serve as the expert. He can be quite no-nonsense, which is one of the things that makes for a great astronaut. However, he couldn't wrap his head around how the can phone would work.

"Where does it plug in?" he asked me in all seriousness.

"It's pretend," I told him.

"No, it has to be plugged in."

Ron simply wanted to make sure the other end of the string was properly attached to something. It didn't matter if nobody would see it. He's a man of details. This only made me love him more.

I asked him every question I'd ever wanted to ask an astronaut, and he answered. We talked about brushing your teeth in zero gravity, getting sick in space, listening to music, and whether he believed in aliens. (He hasn't ruled out the possibility.) Most of all, we talked about the dizzying view of this planet from far away and what that does to shift your thinking. Ron doesn't believe everyone has to go to space to get or to live with this orbital perspective. He feels it's a choice. We decide to see artificial divides between people or we decide to grow and see the humanity in every person.

"One of the key things going to space provided us all, as humans, is a view of ourselves, which shows the reality. That reality

is this: We are one people on one planet traveling toward a common future," said Ron with a strong smile. Fiercely optimistic, he talks about our planet as if we all have vital puzzle pieces each person needs. Our shared problems could be solved if we'd just stop separating ourselves from the very people who have pieces of the puzzle we need. We are not one another's competition, we are one another's puzzle pieces.

Ron is passionate when he talks about the future. However, he doesn't just talk about his future or my future. It's always our "collective future." "Whether you're a child or an adult, the truth doesn't change," he says. "We have a shared future. If we don't learn to work together, that shared future will not be as positive as it could be."

The idea of a shared future is exciting, but it's also sort of terrifying. We might be struggling to handle our own individual problems and our own individual growth. How are we supposed to handle the collective growth of all humanity? I get nervous eating with a fork sometimes, and I've been wrestling with anxiety over how I'm going to be a good parent for my children. Should I be allowed to be in charge of everyone else's future, too?

The shared future doesn't always look bright. We're bombarded with these visions of a worst-case-scenario time to come. The problems around us can seem too daunting, and our abilities can appear too limiting. It can start to feel like there's little difference any one person could make.

I have to tell you, I started looking back at the Listening Tour and the enormous world it revealed to me of schools and educators, of young and old. Zooming out opened my eyes to a world of possibilities, and I truly began to live with radical amazement at all of life. But I do have to admit that it also made me feel really small. I began seeing just how big life is and how huge and complex the problems in it can be. Yes, every voice matters, but not every voice is actually heard. Yes, hope is where we are, but what if we're not in the right place?

Wrestling with my own insignificance in it all, I began to wonder, *Am I really doing anything with my little life to help shape a better tomorrow? Am I actually becoming a better grownup? Am I a great future ancestor?*

Maybe one big reason I feel so small is also the reason we as a society can't seem to see a more optimistic future. I think it's because we fail to see any ways we could be a part of creating it. The future has been decided. What will be, will be—regardless of what we do. Ron told me a story that changed all this for me. I have since tried to share it with every kid and former kid in my path.

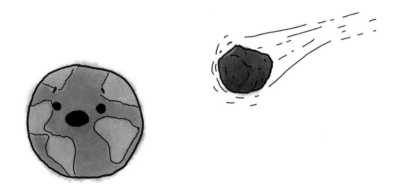

He began by describing a scenario that didn't sound too far out of place for a science fiction film. Imagine that Earth is in imminent danger of being hit by a giant asteroid. This asteroid is big enough to wipe out every living thing here. Scientists have studied it. Astronomers are watching it closely. There is no denying it, this enormous mass of destruction is headed directly for our home. The soundtrack blasts ominous music. People cry. Our shared future is grim.

Now, in similar scenarios like this in films, the story dictates that the government or some brilliant and ambitious problem-solver sends a ragtag team of space heroes to blow up the asteroid. We wage war against the asteroid. Our show of force humiliates the asteroid. We make it sorry it ever came close to our part of the galaxy. There are many explosions. Humans win. The end. The soundtrack blasts upbeat music. People cheer. Our shared future is bright.

That might work in the movies, but it is not how it would play out in real life. Ron explains that it'd be much less explosive, but no less fascinating. With the asteroid on a collision course for planet Earth, we wouldn't throw up our hands and give up. On the other side of that, we wouldn't send space heroes or explosives, either. What would it take? Even with just slight advance notice, we could take action. Here's what we'd do.

A small spacecraft would need to be sent into orbit. That spacecraft would then extend an arm to the asteroid. With the force of a feather, it would nudge the space rock. Over the course of its remaining journey, that tiny nudge would result in hundreds of thousands of miles in missed distance for the asteroid to our planet.

SPACECRAFT NO BIGGER
THAN A SMALL CAR

ASTEROID ON PATH
TO DESTROY EARTH

TINY NUDGES can CREATE BIG CHANGE.

Every living thing on the planet would be spared, thanks to a tiny nudge.

Now, not a day goes by that I do not think about tiny nudges. The little things that completely alter the trajectory of something seemingly impossible to move. The small, insignificant pushes that alter the course of my life and the lives of people around me. Though we might want to do big, grand things to make our mark on this universe, maybe the boldest, biggest thing we can do is propel a brighter future forward with little, tiny nudges. There is radical power in being gentle. One tiny nudge can transform everything.

As Ron told me, "We're going to steer ourselves toward the beautiful, positive, visionary future. It just takes daily nudges." I believe him. Not just because he's an astronaut or because he's smarter and stronger than I am. I believe him because it speaks to everything I witnessed in my adventures visiting kids and former kids. Each classroom was a peek into the crystal ball of what our future could look like. There I saw young people who already held an understanding that we all need one another. I saw compassionate risk takers, fist shakers, change makers, cheerleaders, bird feeders, joy fighters, lamplighters. I saw extraordinary future ancestors already passing on tiny nudges of goodness that'll impact the lives of people they may never even meet.

We need better grownups who can reimagine our idea of imagination. In that gap between what is and what could be, adults should stand passing out feathers. I've started carrying bags of them with me when I visit schools. It's an invitation for kids not only to dream about the future that could be, but to work today to create it. It's also empowering to realize all the ways we can rewrite reality with gentle but steady compassion every single day.

To believe that the best days are behind us is short-sighted. To operate as if things will not improve, nor can they improve, is to give up. To feel like we're marching toward something terrible is to have your eyes closed to the beauty of all that is around us. To provide little loving nudges every day is to do something very big. We're better grownups, creating a world with even better grown-ups. So here's to the future—your future, my future, and our future.

CHAPTER
FIFTEEN

It was a fairly gentle riddle, but it sparked a deep discussion. Bret Turner, of Albany, California, teaches first graders, so he's accustomed to the unpredictable. This was different, though. One day he posted a question on the class whiteboard. It was something he'd done regularly to settle the kids down at the start of their day. Bret wrote:

Puzzle of the week:
I am the beginning of everything, the end of everywhere. I'm the beginning of eternity, the end of time and space. What am I?

"The very first guess from one of my first graders," Bret said, "was 'death.'" He said that an awed, somber, reflective hush fell over the class, so much so that he didn't want to interrupt it to tell them the real answer. "The letter e seemed so banal in the moment."

Kids don't always provide you with what you're looking for; instead, they often give you something better. That's exactly what I discovered as I went from classroom to classroom. A large part of me thought the Listening Tour would be a way for me to help kids feel better. I thought they'd be encouraged to know a grownup wanted to hear what they had to say.

Instead, they made me better.

We swapped seats as teachers and students. For so long I'd been making things for children in the hope that it would encourage and inspire them. Then when I lost my way, the voices of children encouraged and inspired me. Their unassuming honesty, open generosity, and playful curiosity brought me back to the child I once was and the grownup I so desperately wanted to become.

The responses to "What does it mean to be a grownup?" were always fascinating:

"To be a grownup is to have money. They should use the money and buy kids stuff."

"Being a grownup is someone who is tired and has tired eyes. I want to have a dog when I grow up."

"A grownup is a person who works hard at their job and they love their family."

"Being a grownup means to do fun things."

"It means you are more respected by people."

Some students wrote or drew their responses and then sent them to me. Here are a few of my favorites:

One student, Will, drew a picture of me and him "helping "somewon" with the caption "To be a grownup means to be kind."

Another student drew a picture of a shark. Not sure why. This project definitely taught me not to question things like this. Maybe he just wanted to draw a shark, okay?

Then there's the drawing of a student, Samuel, imagining what he'll look like when he grows up to play in the NFL. I love what he wrote in part of his essay:

"To be a grownup means to inspire kids to make them want to be a grownup."

I remember being terrified to ride my new bicycle. I'd had the training wheels off my bike for quite a while, but my dangling legs made known to all that I'd long outgrown it. To remedy this, my parents bought a bicycle for me that was much too big. Like, ridiculously too large for a child. One of my favorite moments of all time, though, happened when my well-meaning grandmother tried to convince me to ride it.

After telling me things like, "You'll grow into it" and "You just need to try it," she moved the kickstand upward with her foot. With a bit of a struggle, she climbed onto the seat. Playfully she bounced up and down and then shot me a devilish look. Without any warning, she took off down our gravel driveway and didn't turn back.

I'll never forget the jolt of seeing my grandmother steal my bike. She had this massive grin on her face and actually picked up quite a bit of speed. I began wondering if she would ever give it back to me. With a joyful howl, I heard her say, "This is fun!" Then the back wheel spun abruptly to the right, tossing her to the left, into rocks and mud. Facedown.

I ran toward her. My mother appeared out of nowhere to run toward her. Her merry ride had quickly turned into a disaster. We were certain she'd broken bones and one of us would have to push the button on her Life Alert necklace. Guilt hit me like a sledgehammer. She'd done this just to encourage me to ride that bike.

She lifted her face out of the mud and said, "Your turn!"

The image of her riding that bike and the giddy way she shouted, "This is fun," is something I think about all the time. The terror I felt when she crashed. The way she then told me it was my turn to do the same.

She's truly one of the crucial grownups I've had in my life.

Whether it was riding a bike or raising children, every action she took, she did so with great joy. Even when the bike came to a crashing halt or life interrupted with any one of its many other surprises, she looked at me and then I'd hear, "Your turn!" As if to say, now you do it—but do it better.

There's a wonderful old story about a man named Andrea del Verrocchio. He was an artist and his paintings and sculptures were said to bring people to tears. His art was so lively and seemed to capture the world around in such vivid ways that people gave him a nickname. They called him "True Eyes." It was as if he had the uncanny ability to see all things as they really were.

When Verrocchio died, people mourned. As people can sometimes do, they began to debate which of his artworks could be declared the best. Some said his masterwork had to be one of his early religious paintings. Still others said Verrocchio's masterwork had to be one of his alluring bronze sculptures. The debate raged on.

Many said his final work was his crowning achievement. Just before he died, Verrocchio spent all his time on an equestrian statue. As he chipped away at it, there were many who thought it was foolish. They didn't see how he'd ever be able to sculpt a horse to look as if it were in perpetual motion. To get this effect, the horse would need to be on three legs. With that one leg up in the air, the piece would be sure to fail.

EQUESTRIAN STATUE OF COLLEONI
by ANDREA del VERROCCHIO

Yet he did it. He solved the challenge and sculpted a horse posed yet full of spirit and energy. It was lifelike, and it was stunning. This was a major achievement. Sadly, Verrocchio died suddenly just before it was unveiled in front of an audience. The brilliant artist was not there to hear so many who said this truly was his masterwork. One critic even went so far as to say that he'd surpassed anything they'd ever thought possible in sculpture. He'd done it. He'd made his *Space Jam.*

A closer look reveals more, though. While he was an accomplished artist, his nickname, True Eyes, didn't come just from his ability to create and shape beautiful art. He had a gift for seeing everything as it really was—especially people. If you were to ask Verrocchio about his masterwork, he'd probably not mention one of his early paintings or bronze sculptures or even the triumph that was his final piece. He'd probably tell you about one of his students.

Over the course of his life, Verrocchio had many apprentices who worked alongside him. These students would help him by gathering materials, sourcing paints, and building frames; and in the process, they'd discover what the life of a true artist could be. Some of the Renaissance period's finest artists—including Lorenzo di Credi, Pietro Perugino, and Leonardo da Vinci—learned at the feet of this man. In all their work, you can see reflected the influence of their genius mentor, yet also their own fresh spins on it. Verrocchio had the pleasure of teaching them what he knew and then learning from each of them as his pupils veered into wild, new territories he never dreamed of exploring.

When Leonardo da Vinci died, many questioned what his masterwork was. Perhaps the *Mona Lisa*, one of the most recognized paintings in the entire world, or maybe *The Last Supper*. Then there were his many innovations in aviation and the understanding of human anatomy. I'd like to think, though, that Leonardo would quietly tell you about a person, or a few people. After all, he'd once known the gift of a true-eyed mentor. He'd flown and knew it was only because someone had helped him fly. Someone had seen value in him. You don't forget that. You pass that on.

Maybe that's the meaning behind these words attributed to Leonardo da Vinci:

"Once you have tasted flight, you will forever walk the earth with your eyes turned skyward, for there you have been, and there you will always long to return."

My mind flashes to all the many young people I've met over the past few years. They're tasting flight, and they won't forget it. Their eyes will be forever turned skyward because they're surrounded by loving guides. Maybe they'll find themselves to have grown very old and yet still keep those eyes filled with radical amazement at the incredible impact we can all have on one another.

For Leonardo, it was Verrocchio. For Steve, it was his teacher Mrs. Dorothy Fisch. For Hedda, it was the committed, caring mentorship of Fred Rogers. For someone else, it's you.

"ONCE YOU HAVE TASTED FLIGHT, YOU WILL FOREVER WALK the EARTH WITH YOUR EYES TURNED SKYWARD..."

— LEONARDO DA VINCI

For myself, it was a priceless mixture of parents, grandparents, teachers, and camp counselors who all showed me what was essential in life. They gave me a taste of what it felt like to soar, though I did forget. Now, though, I no longer want to settle for anything less.

My time with kids and former kids brought me back to the essentials. I'd forgotten that I was born to fly and that none of us was born to fly alone. Hanging on to this truth now, I think I'm becoming a better grownup daily.

Maybe we exist as reminders to each other of what really matters. Grownups reminding children. Children reminding grownups. We are indispensable to each other's growth. Each of our lives is a story waiting to be told, a song waiting to be sung, a spark waiting to grow into a flame. It is the privilege of a lifetime to help each other do this.

It is bedtime at our house. With toddlers, this routine is never actually routine. There are always surprises and stops and starts. That's the way it goes with small children. It's always unpredictable, never boring, and occasionally disgusting.

Once the pajamas are on and the teeth have been brushed, we gather close on the bed. A glow from the bedside lamp illuminates the room with just enough light to read a story. As my wife and I settle our little joy rebels into bed, I reveal that I've been holding a book behind my back.

In order for them to really appreciate it, I need them to know its origin. "Do you remember Matt? I've told you about him. He was my camp counselor when I was a kid. Now he's my friend."

The kids nod. They know Matt well because he sends them postcards each week. This is a small gesture, a tiny nudge, that's a very big deal to them and to me. When I was a kid going to summer camp, this guy was my hero. I'd since turned to him for advice regularly, and he's remained an important part of my life. One of the many great grownups who've illuminated my path.

"Neither of you had been born yet. I wasn't sure what kind of daddy I could be. Yet he sent me a very special gift. This book . . ."

I hold out a copy of Roald Dahl's *Danny, the Champion of the World*.

Unlike many of Dahl's other stories, there isn't much by the way of beastly creatures or enchanted fantasy elements. Instead, the magic here is found in the relationship between the boy and his father. Though an imperfect man, he and his son journey the bumps of life together. One of my favorite features is a postscript written by Dahl at the back of the book that says:

"What a child *wants*—and DESERVES—is a parent who is SPARKY!"

When Matt gifted me the book, I didn't feel like I was up to the task of being a parent at all, much less a sparky one. It seemed an impossible goal. Yet Dahl's postscript wasn't the only piece of parental encouragement in the book. Matt had taken the liberty

of adding a few words here and there throughout the story. Little reminders to paint a picture for me of who I really was and really could be. As a camp counselor and then mentor and now friend, he'd been who I'd needed when I was younger and was now, yet again, giving me something of unspeakable value.

I begin reading chapter 1 aloud to the kids. They're surprised to see someone has written in it. I let them know it's part of the experience, and so we continue. The book starts with Danny saying, "My father, without the slightest doubt, was the most marvelous and exciting father any boy ever had."

HOW ~~to~~ STAY SPARKY

1. SHOW UP.
2. HELP OTHERS RISE UP.
3. REPEAT.

Then I show them where Matt had added to that sentence in pen: "—*UNTIL NOW!*"

Better grownups help us see things in ourselves that we don't yet see.

They help us wake up and wipe the crust from our eyes. They help us find that childlike joy for living, for loving, for dancing, and for stepping (even on Legos). We discover the world anew, and also our ability to change it.

Whether the people around you are children or former children, may you always be sparky. May people see farther because of the light you shine into everyone's paths. May you grow and help others grow. Love and help others love. Sing and help others sing.

I delight in the hope found in you and me and my children and all little humans who call this dear world home. May we grow together and never stop growing until the sky is filled with people flying and helping each other fly.

Fly and help each other fly.
I'm telling you, it's true.
Fly and help each other fly.
It's what we're here to do.

Acknowledgments

I want to thank:

My wife, Kristi. For the brilliant flourishes of color to the illustrations in this book, but most of all, to my life.

My kids. Thank you for all the ways you help make me a better grownup. The world is already better just because you are in it.

The many teachers, students, counselors, librarians, administrators, and others who welcomed me into their world. At a time when I was uncertain of what to do next, you scooped me up and reminded me of my purpose. It's pretty much what you do every day for countless others, and it gives me fierce hope for the future.

My agent, Erin Malone. You are brilliant and kind and believe in me when I don't.

The wise Caroline Sutton. You listened to yourself when you were a little girl and said you wanted to be an editor. Thank goodness you did. You've been a gift in my path.

The entire team at Avery. Lauren Appleton, for the blasts of encouragement throughout the process, and to Hannah Steigmeyer, Ashley Tucker, Lindsay Gordon, Farin Schlussel, and Anne Kosmoski for cheering this project on.

Sonia Rhodes, the original possibilitarian. Thank you to your entire team and your steady commitment to stirring up joy and beauty.

Karen Myers, Emily Uhrin, Theresa Noel, Hedda Sharapan, and everyone at the Fred Rogers Center for opening your doors and hearts. Thank you, most of all, for continuing the work. Dr. Junlei Li, you are a lighthouse.

Mrs. Frances Hesselbein, Justice Sonia Sotomayor, Mr. Walker Whittle, Ron Garan, Michael Meade, Dr. Malidoma Patrice Somé, Haley Curfman, Catherine Epstein, Bret Turner, Steve Shaner, Andrew Baker, Dr. Alice Wilder, Larry Owen, Bob Goff, Maria Goff, and the many other wise voices who helped show me what it looks like to be a better grownup.

The amazing Novaks. Rainn Wilson, Shabnam Mogharabi, Golriz Lucina, Correy O'Neal, Sarah North, Bayan Joonam, the Shelton brothers, Justin Baldoni, and the rest of my SoulPancake family. Gayle McDonald and the many sycamore trees at Mid-South Youth Camp. Jeff Shinabarger and the Plywood People community. My brother, Matt. Taylor Burgess and the introduction to dear Martha. Kyle Scheele and Andy "Dr. Pizza" Miller for treating me like a brother. Harris III, for inviting me into wonder. The Guggenheim Museum for not arresting Kristi and me. The good people of Henderson, Tennessee, and our church family at Jacks Creek. James Victore, Ryan O'Neal, Matthew Luhn, Emily Arrow, Penny Hunter, and my fourth-grade teacher Mrs. Debbie Perkins.

Finally, my grandmothers, Wilma and Ann, and my parents, Billy and Terresa: Thank you for flying and helping me fly.

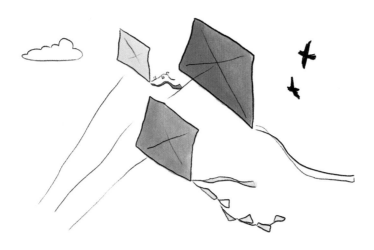